CHANGE YOURSELF
CHANGE THE WORLD

TRANSFORM YOUR LIFE FROM FEAR-BASED LIVING TO CHOOSING LOVE AND SEEING MAGIC

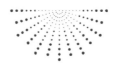

ATOUSA RAISSYAN

AMA PUBLISHING

Disclaimer

I am not a medical doctor or licensed therapist. Persons viewing the content of this book must understand that I am not a doctor or a licensed therapist, and I am not providing medical advice or replacing conventional medical diagnoses or treatments that have been given by your doctor or medical professional. And if anyone feels they need help to seek and/or consult their physician, they should do so.

I am providing guidance and advice based on my certifications, life experience, and practices with my clients for the past twenty years.

FRONT COVER

The front cover of this book is an augmented reality art, which means it will come alive and move.

To see the augmented reality art, please search for and download the free Artivive App. And follow the app instructions to allow camera access. Once installed, point the back facing camera of your device to the cover. Make sure you have the volume turned on. Enjoy.

CONTENTS

INTRODUCTION

If you are like most people, you want a loving relationship, good kids, a perfect job—or maybe even retirement—a six or seven figure salary, a perfect body, or happiness in your marriage and life. You have been clicking on every social media pop-up that tells you how to manifest your perfect body and relationship, get the money or job you want and be healthier and happier. Every day you are bombarded by videos on how to improve something. There are so many gadgets, apps and pills promising a better version of you. It's exhausting and overwhelming!

Many of us have suffered or are suffering physical and emotional issues. It has become normal in our society to have a list of ailments, such as anxiety, depression, gut issues, thyroids, ADD, ADHD, high cholesterol, blood pressure, diabetes, and various skin disorders. The idea that life is about suffering, supposed to be hard and "I must work hard at life" has been engrained in our DNAs.

We've been living our lives following someone else's rule book and therefore plan. Fear has been the main character in our story. We've been living life based on others' expectations and have lost touch with our truth, which is drenched in love. Almost everyone is walking with a hole inside and trying to fill it up.

You may be thinking the key to feeling whole again is somewhere outside and therefore seek various forms of medicine to alleviate the pain, suffering, and stress of life and use apps and gadgets to help you sleep and meditate. Words like narcissists, empowerment, victim, cutting cords, ancestors, and generational trauma have become part of normal conversations. Most of us are looking for that magic pill or silver bullet to make us feel whole and happy as quickly and easily as possible. Sure, these can help, but for how long?

None of the solutions will work if you are not willing to walk the path of healing and self-discovery and sit with discomforts, emotions, and old wounds to discover the truth of who you are. If you want to feel whole, want to love and be loved, want to feel empowered and at peace inside, then the answers cannot be found outside of you and the process cannot be fast tracked.

The answers lie inside of you; the influencers, experts, and instructors only share their experiences and journey and what has worked for them. YOU are still the one that must walk the path, decide what will work for you, and be willing to go inside and discover your truth. The deeper you are willing to go, the more you will shed, release, and heal and find out about yourself. Deep within is where you find the truth beyond your desires of relationship, money, status, titles, and recognition. Deep inside, you will discover to love yourself, life, and move and flow with the flow of life.

I guide clients to see and discover what is hidden inside and learn to communicate with their many different identities/personas and communicate with their bodies. I support them in their self-discovery and healing journey. The more you shift, the more your outside world will shift as well to match it.

Asking the outside to change so that you can change will only fuel your fears. Asking people, situations, and circumstances to change means that you are not trusting life and are afraid to let go of control. You want proof before you are willing to open up, for example, *once I have a different job I will--, once I have the money, I will--, I need a partner to --.*

Your outside world will shift when you realize and discover that everything you want and are asking for is already inside of you. You are asking for a partner to love you and share in your life but that cannot happen when you are not willing to be fully loving and kind to yourself and enjoy your life. If you have a fear of abandonment and fear of loss, your relationships will mirror the same. Once you are aware of your hurts and fears inside, then you let go of them and open up. Once you love yourself and are not afraid of abandonment then your relationships will mirror that love and partnership back. You want money, yet inside you are carrying energy of "not having enough" "not being enough." You carry many fear-based beliefs about money and how money can come to you. Once you let go of your fears and recognize that you have enough, you are enough, and you are abundant then you open new channels for receiving abundance, including money and work.

Once you shift on the inside, the outside will shift to match it. The fear stops you from receiving, and once you let go of it then you let go of your safety shields and therefore are open to receive all that you desire.

The answers are not all found by attaining knowledge but rather in the energy of it all— energy that has been passed down from generation to generation, which you are holding on to because of your life experiences and trauma. Your words (spoken and unspoken), actions, reactions, and thoughts are carrying energy. The outside world is mirroring it so you can recognize your truth and shift. The energy never lies. I don't want you to get too concerned or bogged down with good, bad, positive or negative energy. Energy, like water, flows and has many forms and takes the shape of its container. And just like water it can also change the shape/form of things.

Clients often say things like "I have forgiven" "I love myself" "I do feel loved" and "I am doing this because it feels good." But in their words, actions and thoughts, they have not truly forgiven or do not love themselves or feel loved. They are doing most things for recognition and to be seen. And at the same time a part of them is working hard not to be seen due to fear and what it would mean for others to really see them. The energy is important. You can reframe things mentally or emotionally, but if energetically you are holding on to things passed down or otherwise then it is still within you. I can say I look good but if every time I look in the mirror I see someone I don't like or if my words and actions express that I feel ugly then I am not carrying the energy of "I look good."

Many of my clients come to me either looking for the magic bullet to give them the money, relationship, title, and status or because they are tired of their physical and emotional conditions that do not seem to go away no matter what they have tried. They come because they are tired and frustrated and want a lasting change. You cannot run away from the truth for too long. At some point even if you get all the things that you THINK you wanted (a picture-perfect relationship, family, job, home, etc.), if it has been built on a shaky foundation, it will shake and crumble with the slightest breeze. And the crumbling will happen to wake you up to your truth, the truth of who you are beyond this physical experience.

Getting assistance on your path is great and recommended because we can all use the help. Whether you recognize it or not, help is always there and is being provided and you are always being guided. The more you follow your heart and your intuition, the easier you see and recognize the guidance being provided. Even if you are not, don't worry, you are still being guided. The difference is in the ease of receiving and flowing with life. The more heart-centered you are, the easier you receive the guidance and flow with life and vice versa.

In my early twenties, I always wondered how the gurus and spiritual teachers got to the place of Zen. And as life became more challenging, I found myself saying that they could achieve that Zen state of being because they did not have responsibilities and commitments—they did not have families, kids, or jobs; they did not need money because they didn't live in the so-called real world, and had no mortgages, car payments, loan payments, or credit card payments. Intuitively I knew it was possible and that there was more to this life than the reality I was perceiving. Even with the traumas that I had endured and the responsibilities and commitments of real life, I could achieve the same Zen. And I have done just that.

I have come to a place where life is not about having things be perfect but rather life is perfect just as it is and everything is a gift. Even if it challenges me and feels uncomfortable, it is still perfect because it has a purpose. And that purpose is always for me to release the fear and move deeper in love. I have come to a place where I flow with the flow of life. Love, joy and peace are within me and surround me. And every day I experience gratitude for all of it.

I have taken the teachings of Rumi, Mooji, Ribhu Gita, Louise Hay, and Osho, my energy healing and shamanic training as well as what I have learned and developed over the years and have put it together in this book.

My goal is to help you shift your reality to find and align with the divine that lives within all of us—which is pure unconditional love. And from that space, life is created experienced, and flows. This book provides the guidance and tools for you to shift from fear to love. To heal, release and forgive the past. And to transform your life to love and accept yourself, your life and the life of those co-creating with you.

This book provides the guidance and tools to:

- Begin to release your fears
- Discover yourself,
- Live more aligned with your heart,
- Recognize your choices in your life,
- Recognize the oneness with love in your heart,
- Recognize the connection with everything around you,
- And see a life that is full of magic and this amazing woven plan.

I want you to become aware of your fear and how it is controlling your life. Fear has caused separation in our world, society and in ourselves. To heal and transform our world, we must begin individually releasing the fears and walls we have created to keep ourselves safe and once again see ourselves as whole and one with everything.

I want to remind you that you are bigger than this so-called "reality." If you shift and start to see yourself and your world differently, then the ripple effect of your shift will shift others as well. Seeing yourself and life through a loving and accepting lens will help you to see the world through the same lens. If you start to trust yourself and the flow of life, you'll not be controlling life but allowing the flow. You'll start to see everything that happens as a gift and lose the judgments and meaning of good and bad. As a gift, everything is good and for a purpose.

We are always surrounded by love and most time we are not recognizing how much love is flowing to us and around us.

All it takes is an openness to connect to your own heart and in turn open it to fully love and receive.

I get asked a lot, "Is it possible to fully and truly love yourself and others?" YES. "Can you be joyful and peaceful all the time?" YES. "Can life be really good all the time?" YES.

I can say yes to these questions because I transformed my life from fear-based living to love-based living. From feeling unloved by everyone and the Universe to fully loving myself as well as everything and everyone that comes into my life. From a life of resistance, struggle, and hardship to a life of peace and joy by finding peace with myself and my life. I recognized that all that shows up in my life is a gift, a gift to move me, shift me, teach me, and so much more. I trust that I AM the creator of my life, and I AM co-creating this life and I AM one with everything and no matter what shows up, it's all for purpose, even if it is challenging to shed more.

I want to show you that it is possible to Transform Your Life. It is possible to Transform Your Reality. It is an everyday and every moment choice to let go of fear and be grounded in unconditional love that is always within you and surrounds you.

To "Transform Your Reality," is to go beyond the physical and allow the non-physical part of our universe to merge with the physical and bring about magic and miracles that are always available to every one of us.

There is a mystery in this amazing life and universe that we cannot see with our physical eyes. We cannot feel it with our physical skin or know it with our physical mind. Knowledge will not get you there. It's a knowing that is recognized and felt in the heart and can only be seen with the eyes of the heart. We are all part of this mystery. We have co-created it together and are living it. The attachments to the physical have made us lose or forget our connection to the non-physical. This connection to the non-physical is what brings about magic and miracles into the physical experiences.

So how do we start to recognize this connection to the non-physical part of life? Trust. Trust is an everyday choice. It's a choice of fully taking responsibility for life and what you want to create. It is a choice to see the magic, to love yourself, accept yourself, forgive yourself and others, let go, surrender, and appreciate life and all that it brings you. A choice to be a unicorn in this so-called real life.

Yes "choosing to be a unicorn" because it takes being different and standing out and choosing to step away from the social, ancestral, and community norms, and releasing the rule book. To trust yourself and the Universe. Trust that you are always safe and moving with the flow of life will take you to your destination whatever it may be for you. Step back, allow the flow and embrace the magic.

I can tell you firsthand that once you let go of your fears and control of your life, then your experiences will be delicious and even orgasmic at times. You will be crying just because of overwhelming feeling of love and gratitude in your heart. You will be walking in nature and it'll feel like the colors are vibrant and everything from the wind to the trees and birds are connected to you. You will sit with someone and without saying a word you'll both cry happy tears because of the recognition of love and joy in your hearts. This is coming from someone that seemed to have been born with PTSD, someone that was controlling life, absolutely fearful of everything, and held on to so much that turns the knuckles white. I did not show outward signs of obsessive-compulsive disorder but the way I handled life was with a great amount of OCD. So, if I can do it, you can too.

We've all been carrying a rule book that is a compilation of what has been passed down from previous generations, what we have created over the years based on our life experiences and those of society. All these rules have one thing in common: they are all based on fear. Your parents, grandparents, and ancestors, due to their circumstances, life experiences and to feel safe created rules through their actions, words, and way of living. They set these rules to survive their traumas, and now these rules have been carried forward to you. You are either consciously or unconsciously following them in your daily life. I'll explain more about this in later chapters.

Then there are societal and community rules that we all follow based on the fear of not being accepted and as part of our survival. As you will see in the following chapters, being part of a tribe or community was necessary for survival and social acceptance. The last set of rules are created as part of your own experiences and traumas. You may have created these so that you would feel loved and accepted and as a survival mechanism. All these rules are mainly rooted in fear of being alone and fear of loss. The rules run very deep in our programming since we have tied them to our basic survival needs of food, shelter, and clothing.

Our true nature is unconditional love and a deep connection and trust in the Universe. Since these rules are all fear-based, they go against our true nature, which is love. By connecting with our true nature, love, then it is easy to let go of all the rules.

And when you are connected to love and see yourself in everyone and everything, you begin to recognize "I AM." I AM the lover and beloved. I AM love and the observer of it all.

And I am here to invite you on this journey and guide you to discover your true self.

> *I come to you shining the light*
> *Parting the path to heaven*
> *Yes it may cut*
> *It may bruise*
> *It may hurt*
> *But it will lift*
> *It will bring joy*
> *It will bring love*
> *I guarantee if you trust*
> *You will clear your path for good*
>
> *Life is calling you*
> *I'll keep shining the light*
> *For you to heal and clear the path*
> *to remember you are supported in the wings of grace*
> *to see the heaven inside*

The light is within
Just be a witness
To hear and see
I'll guide you
And will be with you every step of the way

By clearing and letting go of layers of self
I can see the light
The light is inside of me
I am perched in the wings of grace
I am safe
I am supported
I am loved
I am love
I am grace

— ATOUSA RAISSYAN

> *To be creative means to be in love with life. You can be creative only if you love life enough that you want to enhance its beauty, you want to bring a little more music to it, a little more poetry to it, a little more dance to it."*

— OSHO

How do you love life if you don't even love yourself? That has been my journey.

Your task is not to seek for love, but merely to seek and find all the barriers within yourself that you have built against it."

— RUMI

The journey to loving myself fully and unconditionally began the year I was born, 1972, in Iran. I grew up in a culture and family where creativity was never encouraged, and the focus of life was being the best—richest, smartest, prettiest, and most adored. Everything was about being more, because you were never good enough as you were. Even creativity could not escape—if you are going to be creative then you must be best at creating and not just create for the simple joy of creating. This type of environment is well suited for creating a life that is beautiful and dazzling on the outside but empty and unfulfilling on the inside.

Life, being our best teacher, will insist on our soul to shine, creating a radiant and fulfilling life. And to awaken you to your soul's intentions, life hands you intense training in the form of traumas and experiences. For me, this training came in the form of a broken family, an abusive father, Iran's Revolution, the Iran-Iraq war, growing up in a very male-dominated culture, moving to the US, and being in an abusive marriage that ended in divorce.

My parents divorced when I was two. My early childhood memories are that of a struggling single mom, financial hardship, and witnessing her emotional, mental, and physical pain. Then there was my abusive father, who seemed to be amused by his mean-spirited comments and jokes. I was under the impression that he wanted a boy, and he got me, and since his first child, my sister, was a girl as well, he was dissatisfied. In my culture, part of a generational mentality, having a son to bear the family name and move forward the family legacy is a gift and an achievement. To put it into perspective, in most households, from the time the son is born, they call him "golden penis" signifying their importance in the family and society. Of course, they make it out to be a joke, and it's a joke with buried truth.

My dad often would make fun of my body and the way I looked. When I was five, he told me I looked like a boy and that I had hairy legs and I should shave. Sometimes he would add a little torture to the mix. At age eight, my dad was drunk so he grabbed my hand to force me to carry a cockroach because I was terrified of them. When he could not find one, he made me carry a dead one instead.

When I was six, the Iranian revolution started, moving Iran from a monarchy or a theocracy. During the revolution, there were constant riots and gunshots. We were in a state of constant fear. I remember vividly one night being awakened in the middle of the night to the sound of pounding on our door. A man was warning us to get out of the house, fearing the mob was about to burn the bank next door. We headed out running in the street in the middle of the night while looking back at a large mob of men wearing all black, carrying torches, shouting, and chanting approaching behind us.

When I was eight, the Iran-Iraq war started, during which I spent the first four years in Iran. During the war, it was the constant sound of sirens letting us know to go to the basement or under tables to hide, the sounds of gunshots and planes, and the big X taped on the windows to prevent breakage, which added to my day-to-day anxiety.

At this point, my dad worrying about his well-being and future, decided to move to the US via Germany. He figured his chances of getting a US visa would be better if he took my sister and me along, since my aunt and uncle in US had applied for green cards for us long before all of this. However, after his second attempt for a visa had failed, he called my mom to come and get us in Germany since he was going to the US one way or another. My mom figured we were already in Germany, so best to have us stay until our paperwork was ready. At this time, I was eleven years old and got to experience racism for the first time. During that time, the Germans publicly displayed their hate for Turkish people, and we looked very similar to our geographic neighbors. After six months in Germany, at age twelve, I finally arrived in the US, unable to speak a word of English, and during the Iran-US hostage crisis. We were treated with similar racism as in Germany. The looks and words kids used and the difficulties of not being able to properly communicate as a teenager all added to my depression, anxiety, and PTSD.

At age thirteen, I wanted to feel I had control over my life, and the only way I knew how was to get a good education, get a good job, become successful, and have money to gain control, love, and acceptance. And that is exactly what I did. I graduated high school at age sixteen, got my BS in Electrical Engineering at age nineteen, and got my first job as an engineer. Though I was the youngest graduate in the history of George

Mason University at that time, my father's comment when I graduated was, "So what? Congratulations, now you can be a manager at McDonald's. Who is going to hire you?" Another hurtful comment, considering I paid for my education with grants and student loans.

I received my bachelor's degree during the recession, so it was not easy to find a job, especially as a nineteen-year-old Iranian American female living in a state where most jobs were government related. I finally landed a job as a government contractor, writing requirements documents. I remember my first work travel: I was not old enough to rent a car and had to get special paperwork from work. My work was predominantly older White males, which meant I had to work harder to prove myself, not just because of my age and race but being a female as well. So, I went on to get my master's degree. I switched several government contracting jobs and finally deciding to join my sister and her husband in their company. At this point, I had established myself as being a workhorse with an ability to write technical specifications, manage projects and contracts. I was also able to pick up things quickly and would work my butt off. I was always best at cleaning up the projects and bringing them on track and making sure the clients were happy. Around 2001 the company was sold, which meant I made my first million at age thirty. I took some time off to decide "now what?" since I always knew this engineering work was just for the money and security. I went on to become a NASM-certified personal trainer and Certified Master Energy Healer.

Another item worth noting is that, as a kid, there was always a feeling of scarcity on both sides of the family due to generational financial loss and wars. Even if you gave my family millions, they would have an attitude of pauper toward money on the inside, on the outside, the appearance was that we were well off, and we probably were, but I could never tell because of the internal family dialogue. The attitude was that money was something that will be taken away or magically go away, so you need to save and always find a deal on everything. So, money is always leaving and hard to come by, and only a selected few will have a lot of it.

Even society was saying you have to save because you never know! Imagine as a child the stories you hear are all about that fearful day that you are not prepared and there is no one there to save you. The little rabbit that wasted his time by playing and enjoying life during summer and fall and winter didn't have a place to live or food to eat. Oh, and a book that totally F-ed me up, one that to this day I can still remember the illustrations, was *The Boy With Rose Colored Glasses*. It was about a boy who found these rose-colored glasses that made him happy. He would walk around and smile and be happy but everyone disliked him because he was so happy. One day, someone comes to him and asks him why he is so happy and tells him that it is not good to be this happy while everyone around him is suffering. The boy is told that he must share in the people's miseries. He could not understand why, and they broke his glasses so he would be just as miserable. The moral of the story you ask? My takeaway as a child was that if I am happy, I should keep it to myself and not share or show it. Because if I did, others would not like me or want to be with me. And even worse, if I shared my happiness, others would make sure to ruin it for me by taking it away, therefore adding to my fear of being too happy, fear of having things when others around me don't or are suffering, fear of being alone and fear of loss.

Getting back to where I left of, I was carrying a feeling of lack, fear, and generational loss and not to mention, feeling that I didn't know best (adults told me so), and I could not trust myself. All perfect ingredients for me to think "what do I know?" and handing over management of my finances to a trusted "male" figure in the family. In the meantime, I played around with being a personal trainer as a business and provided energy healing sessions for family and friends. However, at that time these activities did not turn into the next "work/career" mainly because I was looking for safety and security and not passion. And being a trainer or healer was more of passion and not a career.

During this time, I also met my ex-husband. Again, another one of those times that I let society and others dictate how I should live my life. I was in my early thirties, and society had told me my clock was ticking on my looks, on my body and especially on my uterus. I was not much of a dater and going out with different people, combined with the fear of running out of time, meant this relationship had to be it. He was introduced to me by good friends, there was a connection, he seemed to check many of the boxes that society, culture, and family had put on the "perfect life mate," so, I needed to make sure this was IT.

My sister and her husband had formed a new company, and when they asked me join, I said yes. My life was not mine—all the money I had plus borrowed went into their business, especially since I had decided I didn't know about finances and managing them. I was married now to an abusive narcissist, had doubled down on the marriage, and was pregnant at thirty-five. The verbal, mental and emotional abuse was getting worst each year. My pregnancy made things worst since I was not traveling at all for work and we both worked from home. The company did not seem to be going in the right direction and I was out of money. After my son was born, the abuse hit an all-time high and I asked for separation/divorce unless we got help, which he refused. My marriage was full of mental and emotional abuse. He would lose control easy and would yell and break things around the house; he threw a glass bowl at me, barely missing my stomach—I was seven months pregnant at the time; he threatened me with a knife when my son was two, saying that he was going to mess me up; he kicked me in the back after we notarized the separation paperwork; he broke in after moving out, stealing my journals among other things and later threatened me every chance he got that he would publish all my journals on social media.

The process of divorce and courts put my fears and PTSD in overdrive. Since I naturally seemed to have a very high tolerance for shit, the Universe answered by pilling up more shit than I could handle to get my attention so I would start to change my life. It's worth mentioning that the Universe does this lovingly for us to release what is not aligned with the life we desire. For us to stop and start going inward and living inward and connecting with ourselves and our hearts. The journey to recognize our true form and nature beyond this physical fear-driven life.

During this journey, my body was trying to get my attention through a variety of physical ailments, some of which were migraines, rheumatoid arthritis, TMJ, candida, ovarian cysts, endometriosis, acid reflux, stomach ulcers, PMS, chronic fatigue, PTSD (marriage/divorce), anxiety, and skin issues. I worked out like a beast; I was doing CrossFit before CrossFit was a thing and could do two-finger pushups. My cardio of choice was running because it would make me numb. But no matter how much I worked out and ran, it still didn't take away the pain inside. I felt unloved, unworthy, undeserving, unsafe, and alone, and a variety of fears. The biggest one being I will end up being old and alone with this very vivid image of me as an old bag lady pushing a cart in the street or alone in a dark house that all the neighborhood kids fear and point to.

I spent my childhood and the first part of my adulthood trying to fit in and be loved. The message I was perceiving/receiving was that if I acted a certain way or looked a certain way, I would be loved and accepted. I had to be smart, pretty and skinny, good, obedient, conforming, successful, and follow the religious and society's values of being a "good" female. But the cherry on top was that I would never be as good as or as powerful as a man. Most of the choices and decisions I made in my life were so that I could be loved and accepted by my family, friends, and society, to feel safe and supported.

There is always light at the end of the tunnel.

During the divorce, all the things my ex was doing, the stress of divorce, my triggers, and having a very young child were so challenging that I could not work. I would sit in front of my computer to write design documents, but I was mentally, emotionally, and intellectually unable to read anything or write any documents. It was as if everything was in a different language and I could not formulate anything to be able to write it down. It's worth mentioning that before this, I was known for my fast turnaround of documentations and for being one of the best employees no matter where I worked. After a few months of battling this, I just stopped. I could not do the work so I might as well stop the madness. I was hoping that a break would either give me enough time to come back and be able to work or figure out what's next if I could not do this job. I took a paid leave of absence. I decided to take out the coloring pencils, pastels, and charcoals that I had in the back of a small closet under the stairs and just started drawing whatever came to me. At the same time, I started reading Rumi again. This time, reading Rumi was different. Now, I was getting the real message. Rumi's poems became my inspiration to create artwork. It was amazing that the more I read the poems, the more images were forming. I also started to do photography, another form of creativity that I had enjoyed and loved but never allowed myself to do.

At some point, I was encouraged to put my artwork online, and to do that, I had to take photos of the art. In the process of putting the art online, I taught myself Photoshop and Lightroom, which opened my art to another whole beautiful world of possibilities. I soon began to create digital art, which made it easier for me to express what I was feeling and seeing. As I was creating my artwork, I received messages. Soon I was formulating my own words and poetry as inspirations for the artwork.

A door had opened, the messages, like instruction manuals, were flowing to me, and each time I would get to see and release layers of myself. Eventually, the deadline to go back to work or quit approached and I chose not to go back, still full of fear of survival as a single mom with a very young child, yet with my whole heart and body I knew I could not go back to the engineering world. I had opened myself up to receiving, so the Universe used everything to send me messages and guide me.

I was sending out resumes to every non-technical position that I could think of and changed my resume in ten different ways, but was not getting any responses. I continued to use my training as a Master Energy Healer along with other tools that I was receiving and formulating to become aware of my layers, heal them and release them.

As more layers were being released, the lessons would become more challenging. The surface layers are easy to get to, but for where I wanted to go, I needed deeper dives, and the deeper you go, the tougher it becomes to see, heal, and release. It never crossed my mind to stop or change direction. As I was creating this new life by peeling back layers of myself, releasing and healing, I was also helping other friends to do the same. I got the encouragement I needed to open my holistic health practice to help others transform their lives. I was using the techniques I had learned in healing myself for others, and now messages and lessons were coming in more clearly. My communication with my spirit guides, nature, and everything around me was much stronger and clearer.

I also started getting messages about looking into shamanism. As soon as I found my shaman mentor, everything clicked. It was reassuring to see that what I had learned on my own and was practicing was what I was being taught. Part of my healing journey was to gain confidence and trust in my knowing and working with my mentor allowed me to gain that trust. In addition, it allowed me to go much deeper into what I knew and was already practicing. Fast forward to today, I have a wonderful practice and have been blessed to be a part of so many people's journeys, guiding them to a more fulfilled life full of love.

There was a moment several years ago, during a meditation and one of my downloads, when I saw all the events in my life lineup and saw the wonderful map. FYI, a download is when you receive messages and/or information during meditation or a time of connection with nature. The reason behind all those events and traumas, and the way they happened, was to bring me to this time and space. I remember being in awe and feeling an overwhelming amount of gratitude that no words could explain.

I remembered that I was very young and not even in school when I started watching movies of different prophets, which made me want to be a healer and spiritual guide/teacher to help people. When you ask the Universe for something, it gives it to you by showing you what needs to be released. My life needed to happen the way it did for me to learn all the tools and techniques, learn to let go of all my stuff, and relate and help all those that come to me. I teach what I practice myself in my daily life. Otherwise, I would not be a good teacher.

I am willing to see my clients fully, love, and accept them fully, and I am not afraid to walk in their shadows and guide them to the light. I believe that is why my clients have been so wonderful to call me a "Game Changer" and "Best Teacher and Mentor" because not only can I relate to their pain, but I can also show them that if I can do it, they can do it too. I guide them to release all that is holding them back, so they can fully love and accept themselves, trust themselves and the Universe's plan and stand in their power. I have been blessed to be part of their life transformation, and each is a beautiful gift to me.

I stand today more powerful than at any other time in my life, yet humbled and in awe of this wonderful creation we call life; I am fully and completely accepting of myself; I fully and completely love myself; I fully and completely trust the process, even if sometimes gets my body shaking and asks me to jump without a net; I fully trust myself and my knowing, I am worthy, I am connected to an infinite source of love, peace, joy, and abundance; I am loved, and I am love, I am creation in motion.

Creation in Motion:
You are made of the Four Elements,
Of Mother Earth and Father Sky.
You are a miracle and magic,
a masterpiece;
you are creation in motion.

— ATOUSA RAISSYAN

When you think of the four elements—air, fire, water, and earth (metal, crystals, minerals, etc.)—you can feel their presence on this planet that we call home. It is part of the very fabric of our existence on this planet. Now, connect with each one in your own body, air needed for our survival, lungs; fire is at the core of the planet and our core and needed for our grounding and passion for life; our bodies are made of 60% water, and the planet is 71% water; and the very fabric of this earth is running through our veins in the form of 102 minerals that make up our bodies, 99% of the mass of the human body is made up of the six elements that are the fabric of this planet. Do you think it's a coincidence?

Yes, we are made up of the four elements. Our mother is Mother Earth, and our father is Father Sky. We are made up of the planet and the stars. If you are a child of the stars and planets and cosmos, how can you not be anything but a miracle and magic? How can you be anything but a beautiful masterpiece? You get to create life through this motion that is part of the planet, the cosmos, and just the very motion of existence, birth, death, and rebirth. We get to wake up each morning, reborn, with choices to create the life we desire. So, create your life web.

> **Create Your Life Web:**
> *You are the creator of your life*
> *So be creative and patient*
> *When building your life web.*
> *Weave your dreams,*
> *Add magic, add love,*
> *Be gentle and grateful*
> *Trust in your creation and the Universe*
> *For nothing is created without purpose.*
>
> — ATOUSA RAISSYAN

This poem is from one of our amazing teachers, the Spider. As you wake up each morning, let the spider remind you that you are being reborn and creating your life, so be creative, patient, grateful, gentle, and compassionate, create with love, and remind yourself that nothing in this wonderful magical amazing life is ever created without purpose.

I didn't get here overnight. I was seeking from my heart to know and feel the truth that my gurus and teachers had reached, within me and I was willing to do whatever it took to get there. Was this journey challenging? Of course, it was extremely challenging. Was it worth it? YES. Absolutely every single moment of it.

There were so many days, weeks, and maybe even months at times, that felt like the end of the world to me in every aspect. It felt like a black endless void that would never end and I would never come out. I did not want to get out of bed, I did not want to be around people, it felt so hard as if I could not breathe and my body felt in pain, which made it hard to function. Yes, some of it was when I was a single mom with many responsibilities, which meant I could not just lie in bed or sit in meditation all day. There were many days, weeks, and months that I would go to bed wishing and praying that I would not wake up in the morning. It felt death would have been easier to go through than enduring another day.

And there was a part inside of me that felt the light and knew that it had to go through this so-called hell. I chose to go through the hell, that there is no magic cure or bullet and all that I have carried for years, needed to purge and the purge was going to take time.

No matter if you choose to take medication or not, choose to put different labels on what you are physically and emotionally experiencing or not, choose to take holistic and plant medicine or not, the journey is still the same. Your answers, your peace, your love, and the heaven you are seeking are inside of you. And you will reach it.

When I was a child, I wanted to be an artist, a healer, an athlete and as a teenager I had added poet and writer to the list. Today I can say I honor the shaman in me, I honor the healer in me, I honor the artist in me, I honor the poet in me, I honor the author in me, I honor the athlete in me, I honor my thin body, overweight body and athletic body, I honor my curls and gray hair, and I honor the feminine and masculine in me.

In the past, I would not dare say any of these words out loud because of fear of being judged, fear of being labeled, fear of disapproval, fear of not being successful, fear of rejection, and so much more. I was looking for someone on the outside to give me that recognition and approval and badge to be able to say and claim parts of myself. Today I don't want or need anyone to agree or approve of the experiences I came to have in this lifetime. Because who I am does not begin or end in those titles.

I love to create, and I create for the joy of creation. I can be all of it for the amazing fact that I love the words that flow in a poem, book, or post; I love when I see the difference in the work I make as a healer, shaman, artist, poet and author in someone else's life, and I get confirmation of that every day. Even if no one buys any of my art, I would still call myself an artist and would create artwork, because I create it for me. I would put my words out in a poem or story or blog and speak even if no one seemed to be listening.

I am an athlete not because someone said I was, because I claim it every time I go for a run or exercise. I run and exercise not because I consumed calories and I need to burn them; I run and exercise when the athlete in me is asking me to move my body. I eat what my body asks of me and when it asks of me. There are times I have not done any movement for weeks or months and times that I am running and lifting weights several times a week. There are times that I eat more and times I eat less, I honor and listen to my body. My heart is guiding my body and not my fearful mind.

I chose this lifetime and this body for a purpose. I chose to come in this female form to my chosen parents and chosen family and I honor all the experiences as a result. I have recreated myself many times in this lifetime. I had to take responsibility for my life, become aware of all my many different personas, especially the ones hiding in the shadows. I had to love and accept all of me, forgive myself and others and ask forgiveness. I had to honor the people that are part of this journey, by not just loving myself but extending that love to everyone and everything that touches my life.

I had to find gratitude for my life and all the experiences. I had to recognize the experiences of duality to feel the wholeness and oneness with everything. Along the way, I learned to trust myself, my knowing, my heart's guidance, mystery of the Universe, and the flow of life.

If I can do it, so can you. If my clients can do it, so can you. The life you dream about is attainable—I am proof. And it all happens from inside of you to change your outside and to ripple out and change the world.

THE WHY

 I serve the Love and Grace in my Heart so that I may be of service to Others."

— ATOUSA RAISSYAN

The why is simple. I want others to feel the love joy and peace I feel inside no matter what the outside looks like. And if I can get you there, then all the people that you encounter start to shift as well. And through this ripple effect, we can all co-create a different world, a different reality, not just for ourselves but also for the generations that follow.

I want to invite you into a world of magic and possibilities. To go beyond the reality of life into the unreal and unseen. To let go of what is considered permanent and invite you to play and create. The only permanence in life is that you are born and at some point, there is an end to this physical body, death. In between birth and death, there will be many beginnings and endings. Once you remove the attachment to permanence, then you get to have fun play and create.

I want you to let go of fears and doubts and operate from a place of love and trust and from that place you get to see and feel an abundant world, full of possibilities. To go beyond the world of duality and come into the oneness of life and creation. I want you to realize that **you are not alone, you are always connected, in every moment you get to create your life, and you are MAGIC.**

Recognize you are beyond this physical body and physical reality, that you are creation in motion, feel your connection to the world around you, let go of control and allow the flow of life to take over. You are the creator.

You are not alone in your emotions, experiences, and thoughts—different stories perhaps but similar emotions, thoughts, and behaviors. Everyone is operating from a place of wanting to be safe, loved and accepted. Then you have fear of not receiving these desires. Anytime you are triggered because you don't feel safe, loved and accepted, the feeling of fear comes out and sometimes you express it as anger so that you keep others out. Whatever stories you have experienced growing up are the cause of your triggers. The emotions and thought processes of triggers are similar, but the story or experience might not be the same.

One keynote here is that two people can grow up in the same household but have very different reactions and triggers. And the reason for this is that everyone is looking at life through their own eyes and therefore their perspective, which will never be the same as someone else's.

We are all also connected through energy. Through the unseen world, beyond the "reality." Some people are more connected to this unseen world, especially children. When we are very young, we are still more connected and sensitive to the ethereal world. For those that are more sensitive to the ethereal world, they feel things more deeply and therefore the feelings are more exaggerated. There is an exaggerated fear of being different and not being accepted and loved.

The good news is that because more people are waking up to this connection and it is being talked about more so than in the past, it has become safer to have such experiences:

- The energy of a room or place changing your mood as you walk in
- Seeing repeated numbers
- Experiencing other energy forms
- Feeling like you leave your body in the dream state, although you know it's not a dream and you are still physically in bed
- Knowing when things are about to happen before they happen
- Having emotional release with songs and music as if speaking to you directly

We are all magical light beings in these physical forms experiencing and experimenting with life. We came into physical form forgetting our true essence and connection to the source for the purpose of creation. Now that you have forgotten what happens?

You are XX years old and have all these emotional triggers, traumas, relationships, and job and are fully immersed in real life NOW WHAT? Well, Universe is always trying to guide you to feel, connect and align with your truth (higher consciousness, divine self, light form, soul, etc.). Because from that place, triggers are not bothersome, traumas are healed and forgiven, relationships are from a place of unconditional love and acceptance, you feel your choices and know you always have choices and you move through your life making choices that are aligned with you, i.e., heart-centered and feel easy.

You are always being guided to the source, to "I Am." The place where separation from your true essence and the source ceases to exist and therefore love replaces fear. It's more than knowledge or feeling. Realizing you are one with everything, all is a part of you and the totality of it all is you as well. Being centered in the now rather than what happened in the past or what is to come. To realize you are beyond duality and reality and one with everything that exists. And there is no separation.

This book is a map to help you explore. I want to give you tools and techniques to use every day to heal, release and transform your life and the lives of those around you through connection and begin to be aware of wholeness and oneness.

The why is simply to create a new world through the ripple effect and create Avalon, Atlantis, and Heaven on Earth. To create a world where we are all ruled by love and live in peace and harmony.

2
HISTORY OF FEAR

The history described in this chapter is taken from a written history of our world. There are other ideas about Atlantis, Avalon, and extra-terrestrials that I did not discuss here since the purpose of this book is to heal the reality that a majority share and have in common. Everything in this chapter is centered around the recorded history of our world.

Throughout history and civilizations, especially long before the so-called modern world took over, more people believed in plant medicine, in the unexplained world and the mysteries of the universe. They were more aligned with higher self/consciousness and connected to nature. They approached life in alignment with the laws of nature and lived in supportive loving communities.

What happened? And how do we get back to our true nature?

To understand the "what" we need to know the "how" and "why" as well. Duality is spoken about in spiritual doctrine and different religions—good and bad, right and wrong, good and evil, and light and shadow. For the purpose of simplification, I want you to point all dualities to Unconditional **Love and Fear**. (*Anytime I use the word Love in this book, I refer to unconditional love, which is to love without a reason or judgment, and it is extended to everyone and everything. And the closest way for people to recognize this love is love for their pets, love for nature, and love for children.*)

Duality assists us to better experience and understand our true essence and form, which is Love. Unconditional love that is pure and without attachments, expectations, and fear. And from that place then we can easily shift to a space beyond duality and see everything as one.

The goal is oneness. It is to see yourself in everything and everyone and everything and everyone in yourself. To know "I Am." To know that there is nothing outside of the self and break the illusion and separation that the mind has created. It is this separation that causes the fear. To recognize you are limitless, boundless, and timeless. Without the "I Am" none of it would be possible or even exist.

Stay with me to the end where the "I AM" is explained in more detail and you will have your answer as to "How can I see myself in the person that has abused and hurt me?"

To better feel and understand love and oneness, nature and its glorious beauty is our best guide. Everything in nature follows a structure of balance, community, family, order, and instinct. Everything in nature trusts in the world around them, the flow of life, and what is needed is provided for them. The fish has water to swim in, food to eat, and a place to take shelter and refuge in. The bird has the means to make nests and have food and shelter. And this goes for the rest of the animals and plants in nature. Each takes what they need not more, not less—they share in the bounty that is provided for all. They understand the circle of life and creation. They do not hunt or kill for sport or pleasure; it's to provide food and nutrients, which feeds many. The concept of permanent death does not exist because everything is viewed as having a purpose. Everything is part of the same source, and death is not an end rather it is a transformation into something else.

Everything in nature operates on the concept of cycles and the circle of life and that each has a beginning and an end to their life. Their birth and death serve a purpose, and the recognition of oneness in creation. The deer does not wake up each morning with fear that "is today my last day", "maybe I should hide" or "I should play it safe and not be seen too much", nor does the rabbit stay in its hole all day out of fear that the fox or the eagle or hawk will get it. Each one lives each day having fun, eating, relaxing, playing and enjoying life. There is no "doing" in nature because everything follows natural instincts in each moment. Everything serves a purpose in the eco-system, circle, and community.

So where did the humans go wrong? Why aren't we more in the moment, following our natural instincts and flowing with the flow of life?

At some point, humans operated in the same manner. We were part of the ecosystem of life and flowed with ease. In our tribes/communities, everyone took a role that they were most suited for. In other words, each one had a special gift, talent, and skill that determined what was their function and "job" in the community—in modern society, functions such as leader, doctor, artist, caretaker, historian, chef, and so on. Everyone served the community and each other. There was harmony with each other and nature. Just like the animals, we received what we needed and honored the land. We hunted for food and killed only for nourishment and survival just like animals. We honored the kill and used every piece of it.

What is of significance is that there was a feeling of safety and comfort because our basic needs of shelter, food and community were met. The community provided the feeling of love and support, which added to the safety and comfort. We honored the laws of nature and the circle of life.

Just as animals ward off other animals when it comes to their home or young, this was true for the humans as well. Aggression was used in the same manner as with nature.

Historians have come up with the history of civilization by gathering information based on artifacts and drawings, etc. that they discovered. However, a key element that is missing is the emotions and thoughts of individuals and personal behaviors. Fire was the first human discovery to set us on the path of being civilized, and perhaps the birth of fear, since whoever controlled the fire controlled others, therefore the birth of seeking power and the need to feel safe.

Perhaps the origin of fear goes beyond the creation of fire. Maybe it goes back to the first human to be born and feeling fear of loss from the womb. After all, it is very scary to be inside the comfort and safety of the womb and be pushed out into the world. It is very difficult to pinpoint the origin of fear; we can only speculate.

The written history of humans has been based on discoveries and speculations and does not account for the emotions and thoughts of individuals. Without the emotions and thoughts giving us the how and why, we can't have the full true picture since we don't have the perspective of the individuals. Each person's actions are based on their perspective, and it is difficult for others to assess this since each person operates from their own emotions, traumas, and view. One person could be standing at a ledge of a cliff and be excited and happy and seeing a beautiful view while the other standing in the same spot could be experiencing pure panic and fear and not even see anything beautiful. I'll explain more in later chapters.

The instinctive fear is momentary. In nature, when a danger is felt, there is an instinctive programing that takes over in the body. Once it is felt that the danger has passed, it all goes back to normal operation. However, in human society, the fear of loss of life has gone beyond instinctive fear and initiated the struggle of humankind and pushing them toward the need for power to feel safe and the desire for immortality to cheat death.

This fear was the start of the separation of humans, the start of humans harming each other, the start of seeking power and control over others, the formation of classes and inequality, consolidating tribes, creating towns, and so on. Fear of loss is the main fear. Fear of losing health, losing livelihood, losing loved ones. Over generations, this fear has mutated our instinctive program and DNA, from the body easily being able to release it after fear has passed to the body holding on to it and creating different reactions and programs.

At some point, we went from living in harmony with nature and with each other to living in fear. The turning point is hard to pinpoint. However, the events leading up to the first formation of the world's first empire are a major contribution of fear-based living rather than harmonious living. And this energy, along with its emotions, patterns, behaviors, and traumas has been passed down from generation to generation. Those acts of violence have taken away from the souls of those doing the crime and those on the receiving end. As a side note, when we talk about generational trauma, it is not to blame our ancestors, but to bring an understanding of what they have experienced and their behaviors. Each generation wants better for the next but if they have not done the work to release the fear, hurt, pain, judgment, abuse, suffering, then it has been passed down to the next generation, and it will continue to be passed down until one finds a way to let go of the fear and trauma and live more in harmony and love.

From the "National Geographic, Meet the World's first emperor, by Kristin Baird Rattini," the world's first empire was formed around 2330 B.C. in Mesopotamia by Sargon of Akkad. He and his successors initiated the concept of power that commanded obedience, with military force, winning battles, terrorizing, and instilling fear, and therefore their way of imposing order, dispensing their justice, and declaring themselves as the earthly representatives of gods so bringing more fear in the hearts of their subjects and foes.

After all, who wants to go against the gods or their chosen representatives?

Fear took over—fear in the people that felt they were not as strong and have to abide (fear of loss); fear in the families with status and power over losing it and therefore having to keep enforcing obedience; fear of not being good enough or having enough to be able to demand anything or losing respect of peers; fear of not following the norm and face being an outcast and not being able to survive on your own. The start of this first emperor gave way to other emperors being born in other regions to build bigger armies and not risk being taken over. The birth of empires was the birth of civilizations created out of fear and therefore separation.

The bigger the empire, the more fear and force to maintain the status quo, in terms of food, shelter, and peace—needing protection from the outside forces, and the need to expand to maintain power and kingdom. The fear of loss also created the desire for immortality, which also was partly a fear of facing gods and fear of punishment, especially since our hearts are our moral compass and those who commit any kind of violence that goes against the heart, unconsciously/consciously fear punishment.

We have the creation of civilization that started based on fear, power struggles, and fear of the unseen/unknown. Therefore, the creation of physical separation, walls, and borders to maintain and keep out those that are different. Because another fear instilled by the first emperor was fear of the unknown … "be afraid of what is different than you because they will destroy your way of life" or "Fear those that are different because our gods are against them, and they want us to destroy them."

But then as the numbers grow in a particular empire, the need for more grows as well as the need to expand. And when you expand and take over other territories you must show your power by making others slaves and taking away their rights so that they will not have the power to take back what was theirs to begin with, especially if they are different in looks, language, and ways of living.

A great majority of what is happening in our world right now is a result of generational traumas that have been passed down over centuries due to all the violence of wars, power struggles, separation, segregation, and so much more. The trauma that we have brought on to each other and the land. And we have made suffering a normal part of life, and the hate and anger born out of fear are common emotions in that suffering.

Rather than a heart-based, love-based, conscious-based living that brings everything together as one, we have lived a mind-based, fear-based living that creates separation, struggle, and suffering.

All this fear, anger, wars and destruction goes against our very nature and therefore physical, mental and emotional illnesses start to be born and passed down from generation to generation.

Science has backed the idea that the illnesses that are being experienced are a direct result of the way of life and living, from the long-term stressors and emotional triggers.[1,2] The studies show that just as inherited diseases are passed from your family tree in the DNA, it is also true that the traumas that caused the stressors and disease are passed down in the DNA as well.

Therefore, the fear, anxiety, anger, and trauma of wars, slavery, abuse, and abandonment, etc. and the energy of it all has been passed down from generation to generation in our DNA as well. Unless at least one generation has decided to clear it and not pass it on.

At some point your ancestors were on the receiving end **and** giving end of injustice and historical atrocities. The emotions and stressors along with the energy of these activities have been transferred from generation to generation in that DNA along with the illnesses.

Based on Eastern medicine and spiritual teachings such as Louise Hay, for example, high blood pressure is caused by long-standing unresolved emotional problems and not being at peace with the flow. Consider that the blood that is flowing from your heart throughout the body and carrying information, if you are not at peace with life and yourself and carrying emotional issues, then you are constricting that blood flow.

Skin issues are a result of not feeling safe in the world, in our family in our environment and the need to have protection. Our skin is the main line of defense against the outside. It protects our muscles, tissue, bones, and veins, etc. When we are not feeling safe in the world, it can manifest as skin disorders. Thyroid issues are related to not feeling you have the voice or the power to have what you want, not being able to express yourself freely, never having your time and feeling of humiliation.

Thyroids are in charge of producing hormones that regulate the body's metabolic rate, growth and development. Growing up in an environment where we feel powerless in our life may manifest itself as thyroid issues. And these emotional causes are not only passed down but also compounded by our environment.

History of spiritual evolution is also responsible for fear-based living. Early in the history of our world, in the tribal settings, people who were considered to be medicine men and women—shamans—took care of the physical body as well as the spiritual and mental body. They worked with all aspects of the human form. They used their gifts of insight, intuition, and communication with the unseen spirit realm as well as communication with nature (plant medicine) to help the individuals in their tribe. They also brought insight and messages to help guide the tribe. They took care of not just individuals but rather the whole community.

Shamanism originated in Siberia and is one of the first spiritual practices, which included ancestral worship. One of the main points in being a shaman, or any kind of spiritual leader/guide, is when bringing messages or guidance to do so without any of the "person" in it. Meaning the message is not tainted by the way that the shaman feels about the situation, their own feelings and thoughts at the time. It is pure. This has to be true for any individual that bring messages and guidance, to ensure none of their fears or personhood comes along with the message—make it as pure as possible.

There is evidence of worship, gods, deities, and other forms of spiritual practices from 10th millennium BC to about 3000 BC. That time is said to have been the start of the first religions: the Sumerian religion and Hinduism. Most pieces of evidence generally have Hinduism as the first religion. From 3000 BC to 2150, we also have other spiritual phenomena such as Egyptian pyramids, Stonehenge, and other god/goddess worships.[3]

Fear has been a part of the spiritual evolution. As powers of emperor's grew the more the spiritual message being communicated contained fear to keep people inline, fear of punishment by god(s). Perhaps people even feared the shaman/medicine men/women due to their powers of predictions and communication with spirits .

As civilizations were forming emperors and armies alongside, the prophets and gurus were coming to guide people away from fear-based living. To guide to release the fear and know God/Creator as Love and as One and in everything.

A majority of researchers believe Hinduism is the world's first organized religion starting around 2300 BC, Jainism at 800 BC, Judaism at 640 BC, Zoroastrianism at 600 BC, Buddhism at 563 BC, Confucianism at 551 BC, Taoism at 500 BC, Shinto at 200 BC, Christianity at 1 CE, and Islam at 570 CE. Other religions have formed after Islam.

The basis of all the spiritual/religious teachings is the same and that is to guide everyone to the truth of who they are inside these physical forms. To teach that the concept of identity is the cause of suffering and separation from unconditional love, forgiveness, and compassion. In nontheistic and polytheistic religions, the goal is reaching/recognizing the state of enlightenment, awakening, Supreme Brahman. In monotheistic religions, the teaching is similar that it guides everyone to the truth that there is one God (one creator) which is in everyone and everything, and therefore everything is included in the ONE and not separate. Also, it teaches that everything is based on unconditional love and forgiveness.

What all religions have in common is the knowledge that we are all part of the One; suffering comes from our attachments to what the mind has created; and the separation from the source, which is Unconditional Love, God, One, the "I AM" as it is called in the modern term as well as in this book.

However, as with everything else, the translation of the teachings of the religions at its core has gone through a fear perspective. And these interpretations being followed as doctrine bring fear and not love, bring separation not inclusion and oneness. They also teach the belief in the necessity of suffering and a punishing God. Religion has been used as a way for power and control rather than its intention to be a message and guidance to bring us **all** together in love, kindness, compassion and forgiveness.

Our world has been created in fear and suffering rather than unconditional love. With the realization that the trauma passed down from generation to generation is in all our DNAs, how do we heal individually and heal our world?

Luckily there are many ways to get there. And what you release/heal works backwards and forwards and it spreads through ripple effects to impact others. As we set out to heal and release and recognize this state of enlightenment, unconditional love, the state of I AM; the energy of this healing allows a generational cleansing and clears the path for future generations. All you need to do is go inside and only be concerned about getting to the truth for yourself. All else will fall into place as nature and the natural flow intends it.

Here are the steps:

1. Taking responsibility and ownership of your life
2. Awareness of everything that comes after "I" either in spoken words out loud or in thoughts
3. Self-acceptance and acknowledgment
4. Reminding yourself you always have choice
5. Forgiveness
6. Love and Gratitude
7. Trust
8. I Am

The next chapters will go into detail on each of these areas as well as provide practical exercises. Also, please note that this is not a step-by-step but rather a flow, and you will need to mix and match and skip based on what is needed at the moment.

----

1. Neil Schneiderman, Gail Ironson, and Scott D. Siegel: Stress and Health: Psychological, Behavioral, And Biological Determinants (National Library Of Medicine, 2005)
2. Karina Margit Erdelyi, Juli Fraga PsyD: Can Trauma Be Passed Down From One Generation To The Next (Psycom.net, 2022)
3. Wikipedia and Encyclopedia Britannica

TAKING RESPONSIBILITY AND OWNERSHIP OF YOUR LIFE

The first step on this journey is taking full responsibility for your life.

If you are an adult, you are probably saying to yourself *"WTF does that mean? Not only I am responsible for my life but I am responsible for so many other people. If anything, I have too much responsibility."*

Taking responsibility for your life does not mean that you are mature and in control and responsible in terms of family, work, money, success, and so much more that we have put a value.

Taking responsibility is to say I am responsible for my actions, emotions, thoughts, words, and everything else that is happening in my life.

It means that you are not blaming anyone or anything in your life for why your life is the way it is. If you still have not made peace with all the people that have hurt you, caused discomfort, or caused fear in your life then there is still blame that needs to be forgiven. Taking responsibility is saying "All that is happening in my life, is my choosing."

Taking responsibility for your life can be done even as a child to realize that you are responsible for your thoughts, actions, emotions and more important the life you are creating.

Why is taking responsibility important? Because if we do not take responsibility for ourselves and our life then we continue the belief that something outside of us directs how we feel, what we do, how we do things and how our life is turning out, which is the definition of giving our power away.

We came into these physical forms as creators, and in that, we get to create our experiences. You might ask "Are you telling me that I created this shit for myself?" and the answer is yes. And once you take full responsibility, you realize how and why the shit is there and realize and reclaim your power.

Let us look at it from another angle. Say I told you that you are going to come into life, but you are going to forget all that you know, the why, the how, the where, etc. But you get to set clues, messages, and programs so that you get to find out the why, the how and the where. Just like any mystery, the clues, messages, and programs are to be discovered and understood. So how do you think you are going to set the clues and message? How are you going to write the program? How are you going to write the story?

An example from my own life: I knew my shit tolerance is going to be high so I made sure the program and its messages ran in a way that by the time I had collected most of the messages and clues, the shit would be piled up so high to be my breaking point for shifting and changing direction 180 degrees. Had I not set the program correctly and my shit tolerance not been activated, then I would continue to be sitting in shit and not smelling it.

Another way to look at it is perhaps to see life as a video game. Before coming to this physical existence, we were asked if we wanted to have it "easy" and just move up one level at a time without any extra gifts or if we wanted the "challenge" so that we could move up ten or twenty levels and have different gifts. Some chose easy, some chose the challenge so that at the end of this physical experience, they would jump twenty levels.

The point is to shift perspective and see that you chose this life and all that is happening for a purpose, and you always have a choice. The purpose of you realizing that you are the creator, you are one with everything, is to allow your heart to be free from fear and to guide you, which is very different from what society and most likely your family has taught you.

You have grown up to believe that you must protect yourself. That if you go based on your heart then you are allowing emotions to run your life, which is frowned upon. We have been told to fear the heart because it will lead you down the wrong path, and it's best to have the mind be the guide. Take a moment and ask yourself: "can I allow my heart to be in charge of my life?" and see if there are any fears that show up. Most likely the answer is "Yes." Your mind will say, "What if my heart tells me to quit my job?" "What if my heart tells me to get a divorce?" "What if my heart tells me to eat a pint of ice cream?"

If the heart has been closed off for protection or not used fearing the emotions, then the mind is not working with the guidance of the heart, and therefore the guidance is based on fear and input from the outside. But if we allow the heart to be open and free from fear and guided by love, then the mind working with the heart can create from the inside out and create from a place of love.

Taking responsibility for your life is just that. I am not going to let the characters in this story be the author. I am not going to let the actors of this movie direct the movie. I am going to be the author of my life story and the director of my life movie.

Many have heard me say that I am grateful for all the people in my life, especially the villains in my life. Just like any great movie director when you win the award you thank all the people that were involved. And in our life stories, those villains have agreed to play the part of the villain, co-creating with us, which is not a role many people desire. And they have had the most impact in terms of us realizing our power and truth. They are responsible for a good portion of the messages, clues, and programs to awaken you to see yourself.

Everyone and everything in your life is a mirror for you to see you. The real you. To awaken you to the "I AM," the self. When you are pointing the finger outside yourself and blaming the situation, and the other person, and making them the cause for you to behave a certain way, you are giving your power away. Because in a way, you are saying that the outside world has power over you, over your emotions, your behavior, and how you live your life. However, when you point the finger back at yourself and use everyone and every situation to see yourself clearly, to see the triggers, the source of pain, hurt, fear, anger, you get to see clearly the parts that need healing and forgiveness. You get to release your fears, which leads us to awareness.

Awareness of everything that comes after "I" either in spoken words out loud or in thoughts. It allows you to step back and create space between the true self and the parts that are triggered and acting out.

To start this journey of discovery, healing, releasing, you must go inward. The space you create helps with being patient, kind, honest, and non-judgmental with your self-discovery. This is where you will find all your triggers, all your avatars and personas.

Coming into this physical body, in this lifetime, your purpose was known to you. Based on that purpose, you selected your parents, family, and the path and experiences to help you fulfill that purpose. When you are born and as you begin to get older, you start to forget that purpose. You experience your life through the senses, interactions, and experiences. Since you forgot your life purpose then you connect to the physical aspects of life, the reality of the experiences, and in a way disconnect from the non-physical or metaphysical aspects of life.

Another reason for selecting your parents is to heal and release the generational trauma that has been carried forward. The trauma you experience, anything that has left an emotional/mental marker, is a result of your interactions with your parents, family, lifestyle, social economic status, and geographic location. This is part of healing and releasing the generational trauma. We are not blaming parents, grandparents, or ancestors but rather seeing their experiences and why they have behaved the way they have so that we can release the fear and trauma for all.

These trauma markers are how you formed and developed personas that each have triggers, behaviors, and patterns. These personas (or identity characters) are created to function in the real world, to be accepted and loved by others, as well as our safety structures and programs. They are the different characters in your life movie, the many labels we carry, for example, daughter, mother, father, artist, engineer, male, female, bi-sexual, or inner-children. Everyone carries many different personas, which at any given time may be reacting to different stories and scenarios.

Therefore, at times it becomes extremely challenging to separate the true self ("I AM," divine self) from the personas. The safety programs and structures that these personas have developed, over the years, is to keep you feeling safe. And at the same time keeps you in the stories of the traumas and fears. This safety and control are not true since it is based on a false narrative, which is "I am not safe, I have to control my life and in order to be loved and accepted I need to make sure the people around me love and accept me." The truth is "I am Loved, I am safe, all is well, because I AM love, I AM creator, I AM connected to all and the source."

The first part of the healing journey is getting in touch with your personas, and the best way is through mindfulness or awareness.

During my sessions, I see the personas that my clients have created and guide them to connect with these personas and become aware of how they are using these personas in their lives and so to see their choices. Once these personas come into the light of awareness and by you taking responsibility, then it becomes harder for the personas to run your life since you are now conscious of it all.

Awareness means from a perspective of a neutral observer, observing all that touches you and your life. The best place to start is YOU. Everything that is happening is a mirror for you to see yourself and find that space of Love and "I AM."

When an emotion or a thought comes up and takes over let it remind you that at the moment you are wearing a costume from one of the characters in your movie and at this partic-ular moment this character is going through an experience. This way YOU can just stay and observe the character and learn about it.

As you are getting started, be kind and easy with yourself and remember observing is just that—it comes from an accepting non-judgmental place that has no interest in the outcome.

You are simply observing life as is happening, like curiosity, or as if a mystery movie that you are figuring out who has done it. From this place, you are not rejecting parts of self that are showing up but rather inviting them in as part of the whole. You are creating a safe loving space for all to show up.

Also as stated in the previous chapter, awareness helps you take responsibility and ownership of your life and experi-ences. It helps you not see yourself as a victim of circumstances, or that life is happening to you. Rather you are a powerful being that is creating life and everything in your life has a purpose. That purpose is for you to discover you are a powerful being beyond this physical form.

There are many awareness practices to help you stay in a place of a neutral observer. Practicing helps you not be attached to any outcome, step away from emotions attached to what is taking place, not to move in past or future. This can (and should) be an everyday and every waking moment practice. In the practice section of this book, I have provided some good ways to practice mindfulness and observing. In addition, there are awareness practices to help you when you are observing triggers or thoughts.

Breathing in
Breathing out
Lungs Expand.

Embracing thoughts and emotions
As if a crying child
Heart Expands.

Being Aware of body
Grateful for all its functions
Energy Expands.

Seeing beyond the play of
Mind and body
Life Expands.

With every breath
Feel the heart
Feel the energy
Feel the soul
And Expand beyond the physical limits;
Consciousness Expands.

— ATOUSA RAISSYAN

4

SELF-ACCEPTANCE AND ACKNOWLEDGMENT

Most often the challenge of observing yourself or better yet observing your different personas is accepting and acknowledging the persona, its emotions, its thoughts and its story. You become invested in the outcome due to fear. Fear of things not working out, fear of not receiving what you want, fear of not being loved and accepted.

Recognize that if you do not accept this persona along with its story, you are not going to have the acceptance that you are seeking. The persona is a part of you, just like your arm, your fingers, and your toes. If you have a mole on your arm, you don't reject the arm or cut the arm. If your hand hurts, you do not wish the hand away. The persona has been a part of your life and was created by you for the purpose of safety. For it to heal, you must first become aware of it fully and accept it with all its stories of past experiences and perceptions.

Sometimes the challenge of acceptance becomes the judgement we hold. If we have felt judged by our family, community, and society then we are judging the outside world. We feel rejected and therefore we reject others. The judgment and rejection make it challenging to accept, because it goes against the rules you are following to be "good."

Remember, everyone and everything in this movie of your life is there as a mirror for you to fully see yourself in. Recognize all that you are wanting is inside you and the way to achieve/receive it is to first see it in you.

If you want to be loved, then you start with loving yourself; if you want to be seen/heard then you need to start to see yourself fully and hear yourself; if you want acceptance and recognition you need to start by fully accepting and recognizing yourself. It goes back to taking responsibility and ownership of your life and pointing that finger that is pointing outward back to yourself.

Don't seek it out but rather recognize it in yourself. If you are not accepting of yourself then what is being shown to you from the outside is that you are not accepted by others. If you feel others don't love you, then what is being shown to you in your experiences is a reflection and message that you don't love yourself. If you don't feel heard by others, then the experiences reflect back at you that you are not hearing yourself or others and you are not speaking/living your truth.

There is self-honesty and self-truth that go along with acceptance and acknowledgment. It's a willingness to see all your parts even the parts that you don't want anyone to see or recognize. Willingness to see, jealousy, worthlessness, resentment, low self-esteem, not being truly loving to others, judgments, and so much more. Be willing to accept and acknowledge all that shows up without resistance or judgment. You can even take a step further by loving and appreciating these parts.

Accepting and acknowledging allows you to bare yourself and see yourself fully to begin to love all parts of you even the parts that are hiding in the shadows, which brings you closer to loving yourself and others. The parts that are hiding in the shadows are there out of fear and wanting protection. They have built walls and fortresses and elaborate security systems to feel safe and they are comfortable in shadows and darkness and at the same time these same parts are asking why can't I receive? … why can't I receive love? But how can you receive if you are in darkness behind a fortress? How can anything find you in the shadows and bypass the security system you have built?

I see in the shadows and darkness and find the parts that clients are hiding and are unaware of and in a way also rejecting. I help them to see and connect with these parts. Many of my clients are surprised when they find parts of themselves in the shadows or darkness or even in a hole. And they come to know that these parts of themselves are very comfortable in the hole or darkness that they created to stay safe. These parts are unwilling to leave the hole or the dark space at first. Also, my clients recognize that they have not been able to receive what they wish because they are the ones hiding and are fearful of coming into the light to be seen. They don't want love for fear of being hurt or rejected, yet they feel alone.

To receive that which you desire from the outside is to recognize these parts inside yourself and bring them out of the shadows and have them break down the fortress. The process starts with taking responsibility for your life so that you tell these parts that no outside force can have power over them. To become aware of them, bring the light of awareness to their hiding spot, start to accept and acknowledge them and start to break down the fortress.

As I sit quietly, basking in the light of awareness;
The light hugs me and fills me with joy.
My mind, beliefs, habits talk of past mistakes and
*   future worries.*
I no longer follow that illusion, so I bask in the Light
*   of awareness.*
Letting the light hug me and fill me with joy.
My mind's beliefs, habits tell me "You need to move,
*   plan, do, seek, ..."*
"Why?" I ask
"So, you are ready? So, you are prepared?" it responds
I no longer follow that illusion since it is another way
*   to talk of past mistakes and future worries.*
The light of awareness is getting brighter.
I bask in its light, and the light separates me from the
*   illusions.*
As I stay more and more in this light;
The mind, beliefs, habits try to search for any feeling
*   or thought that can pull me out of the light.*
Sometimes it succeeds, but only temporarily.
Since the light of awareness is getting brighter,
*   shining its light and I am separated again from*
*   the illusion.*
The light has revealed the magician that has

*distracted and misdirected me away from the
    truth;*
Making me follow the crowd
Using fear to control me
The trick is revealed;
Fear is a friend to remind me
*Of the magician helping me to see the light of
    awareness*
*And I allow the light to hug me and separate me from
    the illusions.*
*The more quietly I sit, the brighter the light of aware-
    ness shines*
*Revealing my wings, freedom, joy and the space that
    separates the truth from illusion.*
Grateful for the light
I say "Shine baby shine"
I feel its warm loving hug
As the illusions are revealed

— ATOUSA RAISSYAN

5
REMIND YOURSELF YOU ALWAYS HADE CHOICE

Taking responsibility for your life gives you power back and allows you to be aware of your personas. It also brings them into the light to regain their power and let go of the fear and false security by accepting and acknowledging the persona and all that goes along with it. This helps to recognize you are not a victim of life but the creator, and as the creator, **there is always choice**.

Choice is a very important piece in recognizing your power, especially if you have lived your life as a victim and believed life is happening to you and/or against you. When you take responsibility and recognize and accept the personas you have created in your story/your movie, you begin to recognize that you have a choice. You have a choice of actions, reactions, emotions, or thoughts.

You ALWAYS have CHOICE. You may not like a choice but there are always different choices available to you in every moment and you get to choose what feels the best in your heart or the easiest in being aware of your personas in each moment.

As kids, we start feeling powerless because parents, partly out of fear and partly because of being responsible for their young ones, remove choices and options. Many of the choices are simple, having to do with food, clothes, toys, and activities. Having the kids feel that they have a choice helps them feel they have power over their life and therefore helps them feel responsible for their life.

Most of my clients have needed to heal their young parts with eating and clothing, which has translated into issues later in life. It is important that kids feel they have a choice. The choices can be simple and age-appropriate and should not be tied to specific behavior. The kids just want choice and the power to choose. You could give them a choice between different food types, fruits and vegetables and have them choose, or by taking them shopping and giving them the option to purchase from a specific section in the store or specific types of clothes. You could also allow them to choose what hairstyles or activities they want to do in a day—providing three or more options and allowing them to pick and occasionally having it be their free day where they decide on everything (within reason). Giving them a choice helps them feel they have power over their lives and helps them be responsible since they are the ones deciding.

Recognizing your choices gives you freedom and allows you to see you are not stuck or boxed in. When you start to remind yourself that you have a choice, you get to recognize the areas in your life that you have not allowed yourself any choice. You start to recognize the areas that you are not comfortable seeing choice out of fear (of being rejected, not being loved, being alone, and loss) and the need to control life to make sure things go a certain way for you to feel safe.

When you start to see choices, you begin to gain confidence and your personas start to step out fully into the light. As they step into the light, more fortress walls and protection layers break away.

When you feel stuck, it's because you are not seeing a choice. An example from a client is, "I am stuck and feel unhappy in my marriage, in my life, in my work, and as a mom." The process we went through was for her to take responsibility for where she was in her life and not blame her past choices and life circumstances. For her to recognize all her choices brought her to this place in time and space. Then to become aware of the different personas she was carrying—the mom, the wife, the worker, the tired person, etc. She needed to accept and acknowledge all of them as they showed up. Next was to recognize her choices. Seeing that she had a choice to stay in the marriage or not, and that the choices she was making as a wife and for her home, the choices she was making with her kids as a mom, and the choices she was making at work, and recognizing that all her choices were all unconscious and fear-based (fear of loss, fear of being alone, fear of not being accepted). Then when she became aware, took responsibility, and accepted herself, she was able to make more choices that aligned with her heart. It was also OK when she made a choice that was fear-based because she was aware of it and accepted it for the time being. She did not feel stuck anymore. Of course, I am not going into details of the deep work that we did together to uproot the parts hiding in shadows and bring them into light so for her to see, accept and love them as well as generational healing that took place.

Wake up your intuition and your heart. When you recognize your choices and begin to choose from your heart, you awaken your connection with your intuition and heart. The more you awaken this connection, the more you can flow with ease and in alignment with your heart and truth rather than your mind, which is reactionary based and aligned with a certain persona motivated by fear.

When you start choosing from your heart, you experience a shift and see that your choices create your life story. You start to recognize the scale and value system that you have in place for your life. That your choices have been following an external rule book of right and wrong, good and bad, that isn't really yours to begin with. It is a rule book created based on what has been passed down for generations from family and created based on their experiences and traumas, society, community, heritage, and generational ideals. And most of the rules in this rule book were created from a place of fear and judgement rather than unconditional love.

Everyone has a rule book that dictates how to be as a person, partner, wife, husband, parent, etc. It dictates your behaviors and all the shoulds, have to, need to, and musts in your life, out of fear of being rejected (not fitting in), fear of abandonment, fear of being alone, fear of not being loved, fear of not being accepted, which again it is all the same fear.

Did you know that many people have a rule that they have to be nice and do things for other people so that the other person is there for them when they need their help and support. Some people have a rule that states *the only way I can survive is by having money and money can only come through a paycheck and therefore a job*. A rule that *I must work hard to be better and do extra to be perfect, and when I am perfect, I can be deserving so I can receive*. Then the rule of being good mixes with the scale: "I am working so hard to be good and perfect and this person is not and yet they are getting --, it's just not fair, it's not just." Also, there are many rules around eating and sleeping.

Once you recognize the choices and this scale or rule book then you get to evaluate it based on what is wrong and right for you and what is good and bad for you in each moment. At that point you begin to discard the rule book, recognizing that you are safe to make choices and create the life you desire.

There is often the question, "Well, isn't that considered self-ish? Shouldn't I consider others when making decisions?" You are not being selfish when you are making choices from your heart space because you are allowing and teaching others to do the same. Also, when you are making choices from the heart naturally you are considering the well-being of others as well. Just because a heart-centered (love-centered) choice does not sit well with others does not mean that it was the wrong choice or that you did not consider them. It is simply that a part of them is triggered and now they have an opportunity to choose, to delve inside and recognize that part.

Another important part of that statement is "in each moment." As you shift, you are a new you, the *you* that is today will not be here tomorrow. The *you* tomorrow is a slightly different version of you today and so there is a shift in perspective, and therefore shift in what is right/wrong and good/bad. The *you* from a month ago is version 1.0 and today you are version 1.5 and next week version 2.0. And the more you are shifting and recognizing you are safe and have a choice, the more you will shift to a point that all your experiences are good and all a gift.

Just imagine you as a twenty-five-year-old, how different your perspective is from you at fifteen years old; as a fifty-year-old how different your perspective is from your thirty-five-year-old self. So right and wrong, good and bad for each is different, and choices and desires are different. Love and accept your fifteen-year-old, twenty-five-year-old, thirty-five-year-old and fifty-year-old versions for who they were, and the choices they made based on their perspective, desires, and fears at each of those times.

Again, the more you let go of fear, trust the process of life, recognize that everything in life is for purpose and all a gift, the more you'll get to live each moment in love and gratitude for yourself for your life and all that shows up.

Each day
Each moment
Is another opportunity for new beginning
Like flowers blooming in spring

The messages come
You are not this mind
You are not this body
Be free from it all

The fog is lifting
My path clear
The game is revealed
I am not this mind nor this body

The veil has lifted
Spring is here:
Flowers blooming
Birds singing
Colors exploding
I am born again in mind body and spirit

— ATOUSA RAISSYAN

6

FORGIVENESS

Forgiveness is another main ingredient in this journey. So why is forgiveness so important? And why, without it, moving forward becomes challenging?

The main reason is so that the trauma, the pain, the hurt, the fear, and the anger is not carried forward anymore. When we experience something that leaves an emotional marker that we do not clear out, we not only develop certain behaviors and patterns around it but also build on top of the original pain as we experience more emotional markers.

As mentioned earlier in this book, the illnesses that have been carried in your DNA are proof of the heaviness of these traumas that were not cleared but passed down from generation to generation. Some of these traumas were a result of social and environmental traumas and conditioning, such as wars, famine, gender, class, and race inequalities.

Forgiveness is not about blame, right or wrong, rather it is about deciding not to carry the heaviness of the pain and the programing forward. And we are not blaming our ancestors but rather acknowledging what they experienced and bringing peace to them as well. As to say I choose to release the past and live my life without their fears for me. You release the fear and not carry it. The wars, inequalities, racism, is still being experienced because the blame and wanting justice is still being carried and we are not willing to truly forgive and fully let go of the past.

People often mistakenly view forgiveness as making it OK for these things to happen or giving the abuser permission. However, forgiveness is entirely for your benefit. It is about you choosing to not carry the heaviness, and that you are letting go of the ropes that attach you to the circumstance, to the person, and to the past. Forgiveness allows you to move forward in peace and love.

Self-forgiveness is the hardest part of the forgiveness process mainly because we get stuck in the why. Why did I do it? Why wasn't I stronger? Why did I allow it to happen? Why didn't I tell someone? Why didn't I remove myself from the situation? Why don't I love myself despite this? I should have known better. Why do I keep doing this?

As mentioned in the previous chapter, the point to realize is that each day you are hopefully a new person with a new outlook and ready to experience life in a new way. The *you* that is here today is not the same as yesterday and not the same as the one from two months ago or ten years ago. And the choices that you made in the past were made by a past version of you with different tools and perspectives.

Let's break it down in an example. I blamed my dad for wanting a son and for his abusive behavior toward me. I blamed him for not loving me no matter how hard I tried to gain his love and approval. So let's say the seven-year-old version of me had a perspective that she did not have any power over her dad, because first she was a female, second she was a kid and culturally you are not allowed to speak up against your elders no matter what they do to you. And I carried the anger, hate, disgust, resentment, abandonment, fear, terror, anxiety, sadness, and hopelessness, for many years.

Let's take this through the process. First, the adult me had to become aware of every time my seven-year-old self was getting triggered. The awareness helped just be present and see when I was being triggered because of the seven-year-old self and understand the why. The next step was accepting and acknowledging her, her emotions, and her experiences. When seeing it from a neutral observer's perspective, some layers had to be released to be able to forgive: the victim of *why* is this happening to me; the judgmental one (also a part of the victim) of *why* is this a****** my dad and why couldn't I have a better dad; and the warrior that wants to fix it all and save me. I had to be present and create a place of unconditional love, allowing the little girl (seven-year-old me) to break down and just share her story and accept and acknowledge her emotions and her story, then help her to see her power, which did not come from her size, gender, or age but from her choices—and she always has a choice. Then, I took her through steps to see her choices and choose what feels good. And forgiveness, rather than blame, becomes a choice. She

41

chooses to forgive her dad, after seeing her dad as someone that also had his own trauma. Seeing the trauma that had been passed down to her dad from his parents and their circumstances and social and geographical issues of war, loss, fear, etc. His choice was to be abusive to protect himself and not have to look or deal with the pain. My choice and the choice of seven-year-old me became to heal, release, and forgive the past.

Forgiveness most often happens in layers so be patient with yourself. The same scenario may present itself, and you may say but I did look at it and I did forgive; however, you forgave only a part of it. Going back to the example, I forgave my dad and myself in layers: I chose to forgive my dad. I chose to forgive him for not wanting me and wanting a son; I chose to forgive him for abandoning me; I chose to forgive him for not loving me; I chose to forgive myself for not thinking I had a voice; I chose to forgive myself for thinking I was not worthy of love or good enough; I chose to forgive myself for thinking I was less because I was a female and for rejecting myself.

Through this process, there was a layer of generational healing, releasing and forgiveness that needed to take place. My dad was who he was as a result of his parents and their parents before him and so forth. Each generation adds to the weight as a result of family dynamics. To put it into perspective, my father was the firstborn son to my grandmother, who was arranged to marry my grandfather who was in his early thirties. My grandfather was an amazing gentle loving soul; however this was not very true as a husband. When my grandfather was in his thirties, he was a fun-loving young man who liked to drink, party, gamble, and enjoyed theater.

He married my fifteen-year-old grandmother, as was arranged by her brother. My grandfather most likely agreed out of obligation and culture and for being my great uncle's good friend. Neither felt they had any choice because arranged marriages were part of the culture and way of life. My grandfather would often tell us that my grandmother's behavior (emotional outbursts or a delicate meanness) was because of her past and that he was not so kind to her when he was a young man. Both my grandmother and grandfather experienced loss growing up due to political issues of the time, which was a big influence on their upbringing and the upbringing of their kids. Another big impact on my father and his siblings was having a scared fifteen-to-twenty-year-old as their mother, who had to move out of her childhood home into a home with a man twice her age, and still wanting to play with her dolls and toys. Being powerless as a female, fear, conforming to the rules of society, loss of a child, financial loss, and so much more was transferred by my grandmother (and generations before her) to my dad and his siblings, as well as what was passed down from my grandfather and past generations relating to being a man, the war, the revolution, and cultural codes of conduct, etc. What I always find interesting is that by the time he became our grandfather, he was much more of a gentle loving and forgiving soul that did not seem to have any conforming qualities as to the men I would witness in or outside our home. I could write a whole book on family and generational cleansing that took place when I started my healing journey.

There is no blame or judgment of generations, rather holding unconditional loving space for them, understanding the patterns and behaviors. Then forgiving, healing, and releasing the past not just for yourself but the generations that came before. This is where shamanic generational cleansing and healing, cord-cutting, and maybe even land healing is a great tool. Physical land healing helps with geographic locations that have experienced traumas such as war, famine and more.

Be gentle, loving and easy with yourself through the process of forgiveness. Forgiveness untangles the ropes and barriers and walls built over generations and the separation created by fear.

Fear of loss, feeling less, and feeling not being good enough or worthy has been passed down many generations for most people. My ancestors lost their livelihood several times and had to rebuild. They lost status in society, experienced times of hardship due to wars, and so much more. And as a woman, especially from that part of the world, there is a lot that is passed down concerning gender issues as well, which requires forgiveness.

Forgiveness allowed me to have more understanding of my life and my purpose and being able to make peace with myself and the past and love myself fully and unconditionally. To realize my power and remove the walls and barriers and become whole not just inside myself but on the outside. One of the biggest barriers was with my feminine self.

Another forgiveness type for many people is forgiving God/Universe/Life. We may say things such as "Why me, why does it have to happen to me?" "Why is life so cruel?" "Why is life punishing me?" "What did I do to deserve this?" If you remember from previous chapters, life is guiding you to awaken. Life uses every opportunity as a mirror and as a practice opportunity. Everything in life comes to show you your power. If we are blaming God/Universe/life for not just our life but the world, then we are giving our power away. Instead of blaming God/Universe/life, find out what the experiences are trying to show you, teach you. And forgive God/Universe/life for the past experiences, realizing it was all a gift for you to shift and see your own beauty and power, the beauty and power of Love.

Forgiveness allows us to let go and heal. And while you are at it, ask others to forgive you. I periodically throughout my son's life have asked him to forgive me. I know I have grown as a mom over the years—the mom that he experienced as a baby is very different from the mom he experienced at four years old and one he experienced at ten and the one he experienced at fifteen. I always let him know that I did my best and sometimes I have allowed my fears for him to make choices related to him. I sometimes ask him to forgive me for no known reason, because I want his different parts to let go of anything that they may be holding on to.

Forgiving yourself makes it easy to forgive others and ask others to forgive you as well. I had to forgive myself and my choices as a mom when my son was a baby. To let go of the fear and pain of that time and ask him to forgive me, for him not to carry any of it. On another note, don't say sorry if you don't mean it. Do the work so that when you say sorry, it's the truth.

Forgiveness is part of unconditional love. Forgiveness untangles the energies of fear that do not allow unconditional love to flow freely and be recognized in ourselves and others.

When you forgive, you are saying--

- I am not carrying the energy of the trauma forward
- I recognize the trauma in you and recognize your perspective and that perhaps if in your shoes I may choose to follow the path of trauma
- I am no longer bound to you and/or this experience, and I let go and release the past
- I can see you and myself with loving, kind and forgiving eyes
- As I am releasing my trauma and fears, my trauma and fears, may cause others to carry fear and trauma, so by asking forgiveness I can recognize my fear and trauma and ask them to release what they received because of it
- I am ready to see myself fully and recognize the unconditional love (the grace, the god, the I AM) in this physical form

7

LOVE AND GRATITUDE

Resisting and controlling life
Made me blind and mute
Feeling life has forsaken me.

Resistance has broken open
Light is shining through
Revealing my truth;
I have received
All I ever wanted.

Free at last
My Heart is singing
"I Am Life"
I Hear it
I Feel it
I Dance to it.

— ATOUSA RAISSYAN

Love and Gratitude, my favorite part of the book. Because when I recognized that I am life, it opened me up to love and gratitude as part of life and living. I don't have to pause and practice love and gratitude; it is in me and flows out naturally.

Often, I have asked people "On a daily basis, are you loving and grateful for yourself and your life?" everyone manages to say yes at the beginning, not realizing that they are only being loving and grateful to a very small portion of their life and not their life as a whole.

Let's first take Gratitude. At one point or another during the day, you probably bring gratitude for your health your family and your wealth however much or little it may be. But are you truly grateful?

Being grateful means that you are grateful for every little thing that is flowing in and out of your life. You are not picking and choosing, and you are not taking it through the scale of good and bad. And more important you are not grateful out of fear, fear of loss.

Gratitude out of fear of loss is very big for most people. This means having thoughts like I better be grateful otherwise I may lose XYZ. This is a big part of the religious teachings of man and not God/Universe. "You better be grateful otherwise God will take it away." "Be grateful for your health otherwise, you may get sick." "Be grateful for what you have otherwise, God will take it away as a lesson." Even in a non-religious spiritual context: "be grateful otherwise you may not mani-fest" or "only be grateful for what you want otherwise you may manifest what you don't want" And so you are really experiencing fear and not gratitude.

Gratitude does not know good and bad, and it is certainly not related to fear. Gratitude is a natural feeling inside the heart, that naturally arises in every moment. Gratitude is for all that shows up in your life and all that is flowing in and out. Gratitude is associated with the present moment and all that is contained in the present moment. It sometimes doesn't even need an object or subject. It is part of the "I AM" naturally occurring inside the heart and flowing outside for all that is.

Gratitude is closely related to unconditional love. When you ask most people, "Do you express love during the day?" the answer is an easy yes if they have pets or children. Most people have a very easy time expressing love to their pets and children daily. Most times, even that is not expressed out loud or not as often as other feelings and thoughts are expressed.

Unconditional love, like gratitude, flows from the inside out. Therefore, it's not attached to anything on the outside, good or bad, and right or wrong. It's a natural flow that is expressed from the inside for life and all that is included in it. To love is to love the light as well as the shadow, the beautiful as well as the ugly, the up as well as the down. In recognizing yourself, the "I AM," you discover this natural flow of love and gratitude for yourself, others, and all aspects of your life. Because everything and everyone becomes the expression of the divine (divine creation, grace, I AM, God, One.)

For most people, expressing love is reserved for only a select few in their lives and only expressed for those parts of life that bring a smile to your face and make you feel good.

Unconditional love is a love for everyone even those you choose not to spend time with or engage with. Love for those that are different in their beliefs, looks, and way of life. It is pretty safe to say that the majority of people "like" rather than "love", since if it is not unconditional then it is not love. Recognize unconditional love as a state of being not a passing emotion or feeling

Unconditional love does not mean keeping quiet, being a martyr, or harming yourself or others in the name of love. You can still love someone unconditionally and speak your truth. This means speaking what you know in your heart to be true and that it needs to be spoken, not to blame or shame but to speak what needs to be said at the moment from that place of unconditional love. When your actions and words come from your heart and a place of unconditional love it is different than when they come from a place of hurt, anger, fear and the mind. The energy of it is felt different.

Love is for everything in your life. It is our natural form and part of our true essence. And it is not reserved for only the people in your immediate family, people in your life, or people in general, for pets, and your things. I often get asked, "How can you say you love everything so do you love the evils in this world? How can you say love the people that have harmed you?" Easy.

I may not agree and have a difference in opinion and perspective on how things should or should not be done. I may agree or disagree, or like or dislike based on what works and doesn't work for me or rather is aligned or not aligned with my purpose in each moment. However, I love it all. And the reason I love it all is that I know it has a purpose. I know it is there for a reason, and gives me practice opportunities to see things differently, choose differently, or learn a new skill. I know and trust that all that is happening in every moment it is for good of all.

The so-called "evil in the world" exists because most people in the world believe in evil and bad and there is a fear of evil outside and inside them. Once people release the fear, forgive all, and heal all only then the evil in the world will cease to exist.

The big word these days is manifestation, and everyone is working hard to manifest what they want and trying even harder not to bring into focus what they don't want manifested. However, what most people miss is that it is not in the words or thoughts that they are using or not using; it is in the energy that is inside and flowing outside. If the fear is inside you, and if you are unconscious of it, then its energy finds its way outside in your words, actions, and thoughts, and therefore, in the manifestation as well. Since the purpose is for you to discover the grace/love inside and everyone is a mirror for you to see the inside.

If each one of us finds a way to heal and release the past, to forgive the past in ourselves and others, and unconditionally love ourselves and others then all that is manifested is love and in love.

There was a time in my life when I had a belief in just and unjust, in good and evil, in good and bad. The reason for that was that I was carrying judgment. I felt judged and not accepted by my family and community. I had to carry forward the rule book that was passed down as well as add to it so that I would "good" and find a way to be accepted by all. That judgement allowed me to have just/unjust value system that I could measure myself against to know how well I am doing to be accepted. And this system is what I used for the outside world as well. When situations came up that the other party did not play by these rules, anger would then come up. Since I felt I was being judged and had to behave "good" and the other person is behaving "bad" and they are not being judged or punished.

However, I had to discover those parts in me, heal and release them in me, forgive them in me, love and accept them in me. And I was grateful for the discovery since without seeing the light and shadow and experiencing the duality I could not experience the whole and move into oneness of it all.

My greatest growth and transcendence have come from the challenging experiences that broke my fear-based patterns and behaviors and therefore my greatest source of love and gratitude.

Just as in nature everything serves a purpose, it is true in our lives as well. All that is happening in our world right now is to awaken everyone to realize they are beyond this physical form and physical existence. There has been a separation that has occurred outside and inside of us due to fear, and this fear and separation have caused all the wars and injustices in the world.

To shift our world, we must release the separation we have created inside ourselves and release the fear and the barriers it has created against ourselves and the outside world to receive and give love freely, which includes the physical barriers such as borders.

Love yourself, life, divine, God, Source, "I AM," grace, the Universe (or whatever name you like to give it) for creating such an amazing thriller, for self-discovery and for experiencing magic and miracles every day.

My heart is open
The eye is seeing
I am receiving

I have my wings
With no desire to take flight
New light fills this body

No longer grabbing
No longer holding
I let go of safety
And all is flowing

As I float softly
On the surface of River Of Life
I am filled with new light
And fresh life
I wish to become the Giver Of Light

— ATOUSA RAISSYAN

8
TRUST

Trust is one of the biggest practices and the most challenging in life. It's challenging trust yourself and your knowing. To trust life and the flow and process of life. To trust that it is all working out for the best for everyone and everything involved.

Is there a difference between faith and trust? From my perspective, there is a slight difference in the energy of these two words. Trust is implied in faith while faith is not implied in trust. There is no responsibility implied in the definition of faith but there is a sense of responsibility implied in the definition of trust. Trust implies support (having your back), and for that reason, there is more strength and power in the word trust rather than faith. In addition, there is an acceptance implied in trust—that you are accepting what is and trusting what is to come. Rather, faith is more fear- and hope-based, that there is faith in something happening or being provided.

So what is trust and how can you trust in the unseen and unknown? Let's break down trust into trusting yourself and your knowing in addition to trusting God/Universe/Source/Divine. And later there is a merging of the two and seeing that they are the same. When you develop the sense of "I AM" and the sense of self then trusting yourself and your knowing is the same as trusting God/Universe/Source/Divine and vice versa.

Whether to start with trusting yourself or the Universe is entirely a personal choice and what feels easy for you.

Trust in God/Universe/Source/Divine is the same as trusting life and the process and flow of life. You are facing your fears for your life, in your life, and trusting there is more to the experience at the moment. Trusting that it is all happening for a purpose even though you are not seeing the big picture. Trust is a practice so continue to remind yourself of that fact. There are times that you are being shaken to your core, but that is only to awaken you to release all your fears. Practice, practice, practice … can't emphasize it enough. Continue to practice; we are never truly done. Here are a few trust stories to explain the practice better.

"One of my clients' son is visiting his father and calls Mom frantically to come and pick him up. After Mom fails to calm him down, she agrees to pick him. When she arrives, the son runs inside the car, crying and yelling, 'Drive! Drive! Drive!' Mom proceeds to drive and tries to calm the son down. The son is very scared of Dad showing up at the house. And while the son and Mom are talking, they see that Dad is next to them in his car. The son panics and Mom calms him down by calling the police and proceeding to drive. The dad tries to run them off the road. This ends up being thirty minutes of stalking by driving behind them and a few attempts of road rage until finally the police catch up to them and the dad is asked to leave. During the entire car ride, Mom assures her son to trust that it is all happening for a good reason, as hard and scary as it is at the moment. She assures him that she's not sure what the reason is but knows in her heart that there is a purpose and they just have to go through the process.

The matter went to court and got even bigger than what it had been originally. All along, the mom assured her son that was all for a purpose. The court cases were lost and even in that, Mom trusted it was all for a good reason. So after more than a year, the son came out of this recognizing his power in his voice and in his choices, since he had to use his voice many times during the whole court ordeal and more importantly against his dad. The mom lost her fear of the court system, of the police and of losing her son. The son got to stand up to Dad and speak his truth. And fast forward to now, the mom, son and his dad have the best relationship they have had in years, which they did not think was achievable in this lifetime. It was a practice of trust, awareness, choices, acceptance and love and gratitude that helped the mom and son shift and shift their experience of the outside as well."

"More than a quarter of my roof shingles were blown away in a storm in August. I proceeded to do what people do normally and contact my insurance and roofers to come and give me an estimate. My insurance company sent someone to come and evaluate and determine what needed to be done and how much I would get paid. After which, even though it was a very old roof and all of it needed to be replaced, the insurance company said they would only pay for half of it to be fixed and would send the money to my mortgage company and not me. And then after talking to my mortgage company, they proceeded to say they would not send me the check and that they would have to evaluate the roofers and break the payments into small payments instead of paying all at once. This meant that I had to pay out of pocket and then get reimbursed. At this point, the roofers that were supposed to give me estimates refused to do half the roof because it was so old and the price to replace my entire roof was beyond anything I could afford. Until finally I found a company that said they worked with insurance companies all the time and get them to re-evaluate and get more money from them.

It's important to note that throughout this process I stayed in a place of trust and followed the choices that felt right in my heart. And a quarter of the roof was covered by a tarp. After three months of back and forth, it was obvious that this company was not able to do anything and had not made any progress with my insurance. So I began the search for roofers, and at this time I needed some maintenance on some trees and I have known the person that takes care of it all for years. As I was talking to him and letting him know what had happened to the roof, he said that his son's friend that had a roofing company in PA had to move to this area due to some family issues and was starting his business again here. He had three small kids and one on the way, and he could use the job. Right there I knew why things had worked out the way they did and I could not hire other roofers. This person came and gave me an estimate to replace the roof at a price I could afford. And when I called the mortgage company to find out what paperwork they needed from the roofer, they were surprised by the question and said that they did not need any information and they would release 100% of the funds at once and send me a check. It all worked out the way it needed to for all parties involved. I trusted the process and knew it is all for a purpose and was sure my house would be fine during the fall rainy season. I trusted myself and my knowing and allowed everything to flow. It was a practice of trust and choices."

Sometimes trust requires more of us and that is when we have to know and trust that every experience has been designed and provided with love for us to release the fear and separation. In recognizing the "I AM" (Divine, Grace, God, Universe), you also recognize that you designed the experiences and clues and messages to help yourself wake up to the reality of your life that is you are divine and always connected. This is where trust in yourself and your knowing is important. And that trust in yourself and your knowing is that you are trusting the guidance from your heart and your intuition.

When I ask people to follow the guidance from their heart, they are immediately faced with fear and ask what if my heart tells me not to go to work, what if my heart tells me to eat ice cream, what if my heart says take the day off and sleep in bed, what if my heart tells me to quit my job. The truth is your body and your heart know the way and know best what you need and what is good for your and will not lead you stray. However, when we have fear-based living rather than love-based living we are guided by our mind and not our heart. Yes, your heart might tell you that your body, mind and spirit need rest, and when you have rested it will tell you it's time to move. Yes, your heart might tell you to eat ice cream but what it is telling you is that at the moment your sugar is low and you need calcium as well. Yes, your heart might tell you that this is not the right job for you so that you may start to move in the direction of a job that is more aligned with you and your purpose. When you become more in tune with your heart and your intuition, you listen and understand better. And when you are communicating better with your heart and intuition, you understand the guidance that you are receiving and therefore moving with the flow of life.

Trust in yourself and your knowing means that you listen to your heart—even if 10,000 people tell you to go left but your heart tells you to go right, you go right. Some time ago, my house was about to go into foreclosure, and everyone's advice was for me to sell. Not even one person was telling me to stay. The reality of the situation did not seem hopeful at all, and the reality was to sell and not risk foreclosure and all that goes along with it. However, I decided all my life I listened to my mind and others' guidance and allowed fear and others to have control over my life and it is time for me to take responsibility for my life and allow my heart to guide me. Every step of the way I decided to practice trust, listen to the guidance of my heart and follow it. Assistance showed up when I needed it the most and magically things started to work out on their own. Ten years later I am still in that same house. It was truly magical since I don't how I paid the bills and made sure my son had everything he needed and wanted. The money coming in for sure did not match the money coming out. Also trust opened me up to change my life from being money-centric to abundance-centric.

A big part of trust triggers our financial security. So, when I shifted to more of an abundance mindset. Since I was not focused on money, paycheck and job and shifted to seeing the abundance I had in all aspects of my life, then I started receiving things so much easier. I recognized and appreciated that I was part of an abundant universe that flows in many directions (so it is not just through a paycheck and a job) and many shapes and forms (love, magic, messages, nature, money, knowledge and so much more). Every time I went to a grocery or restaurant, I randomly received free things—free leg of lamb, free appetizers, and free drinks. I even received free gifts from Amazon in the mail.

Part of this practice of trust along with acceptance and acknowledgement is surrender. Surrender is not giving up but rather letting go. It is as if you are holding on to a railing so tight that your knuckles are white out of fear and then you let go of the railing and allow what is to happen happen. It is a letting go, maybe even falling backward and trusting. Surrender means stopping resistance and the fight and opening the hands, letting go of control, trusting and allowing the flow of life to carry you.

Try not to resist the changes that come your way. Instead, let life live through you. And do not worry that your life is turning upside down. How do you know that the side you are used to is better than the one to come?"

— RUMI

9
I AM

Come away with me
Beyond the darkness
Beyond the light
There is a space
Beyond you and I
Where fear subsides
Beyond the mind
Where boundaries disappear
Enter the paradise inside the heart
Where shadow and light are as one
Where you and I become one

Close your eyes
Let me be your guide
To this enchanted land
To find the magic inside
Where love encompasses all
All becomes one
As "I"

— ATOUSA RAISSYAN

All teachings of gurus, masters, ascended masters, and prophets point us to recognize ourselves as God, Universe, Source, whatever you want to call it that feels best to you. In this book, the recognition of this state is referred to as "I AM."

So why is this recognition so important? Once you recognize you are part of everything and everyone, you no longer see the separation or seek to separate yourself from everyone and everything else. Instead you see a part of you in them and therefore allow yourself to release the fear and allow the unconditional love to flow to everyone and everything in your life. You see everything as a part of a whole. You no longer feel everything is against you but a part of you and working with you and for you. You are no longer separate but connected and a part of. You no longer fight and resist, instead you surrender.

One thing that I feel I am teaching a bit differently is to invite and include rather than separate. Most of the teachings that I came across made me feel as if I was to battle the mind and battle the self and battle the ego. That there was bad and good energy. The teachings made me feel more as if I needed to resist, fight and force things. However, what I came to recognize when I removed the definition of good and bad and accepted everything, surrendered, trusted, and saw life with loving and grateful eyes was that I was led to see that everything is part of ONE. That I needed to include everything to feel whole and complete. You bring your light and shadow together not reject the shadow. You are not fighting the mind, the ego and the self. Instead, recognize them, understand the *why* behind their behavior and invite them to surrender and trust. Do not reject them, fight with them, or call them bad. Everything—and I do mean everything—in life is part of ONE. It has to be to break the separation created in ourselves and our world.

How do you get there? Now that is the million-dollar question.

The truth is all who seek will find their way. Set your intention to merge with the heart and it will be the moving force on this path. And there are many ways to get there. Realize there is no right or wrong way, or your way or my way. Whatever way your heart is guiding you is the right one for you. Since you are receiving the experience, you need to figure things out. This is not a place where knowledge, logic or mind will guide but rather your heart and love will take you there. And all who seek will get there. The intention is moving you and your heart is guiding you. There are no mistakes.

The steps outlined in this book are what helped me recognize the "I AM." It is still a work in progress, and it is a flowing dance. As I move deeper and become steady in this recognition, all else falls away and apart naturally. I feel it, I live it, I recognize it, and the dance is recognizing and honoring the "I" in this form in this lifetime. I came here to recognize and live this truth as "I AM" and recognize it in everything and everyone and release the barriers to this recognition for myself and others (living and not living). So yes, there are times that anger, sadness, frustration, and fear come up; however, they don't take me away with them. They are either on the surface and easily passing through, or if deeper, I receive them with open arms, knowing it's for purpose and allowing me a deeper recognition of the grace inside my heart

Our purpose for this birth into the physical form has been to turn inside and recognize the "I AM" that encompasses everything as well as being beyond it all.

Before, I took the teachings of my gurus as an impossible task as long as I was living in this reality with my life responsibilities. I even would go as far as saying that because they were all male, they did not have the same emotional structure. However, from deep in my heart, I was still seeking to achieve this connection to my truth while being in a so-called "normal" life. And I received my answer. I have recognized it. This is another reason that I am writing this book to say it is doable. You can and will get here if you choose it, after all, we all have this truth in common. It's a choice to live it or not, to seek it or not.

And inside, it will lead you to your heart, the center, the starting point of it all. The heart is at the center of this physical form for a purpose and without it, this physical form will seize to function. The first thing an ultrasound shows is the heartbeat and heart. There isn't much else that is formed really. This heartbeat is the indication that the energy source (soul, light) has entered into this physical form. And the heart is where you will find all your answers and where you need to seek from. And the heart is synonymous with unconditional love.

The more you move into this recognition and move toward love-based living rather than fear-based living and open yourself up and trust the flow of life, the more you move every day about your life with freedom, peace, love and gratitude. There is a natural gratitude that takes over. It is hard to describe this place, but you understand life and life become beautiful and magical and full of possibilities. Yet you are not attached to achieving, receiving or doing, everything is part of a natural flow and process and in the moment. As you are walking the path to this recognition, you will get more and more glimpses in between the challenging times of purging, and you can be sure that you will be reaching this place of recognition. And yes, the process of purging can be trying at times but it's necessary. This purging time may be physical or emotional, and at some point, some people call it the dark night (week/month) of the soul. Most common physical symptoms can appear as body aches, sometimes flu-like symptoms, digestion issues, headaches, migraines, chills, body shakes, or dizziness/lightheaded and emotions that feel like you are either on a roller coaster or have done a deep dive at a bottom of a very deep hole and can't seem to find a way out. Rest assured they are all temporary and will pass. Be kind and easy with yourself and find ways that will help ease it in each moment, from mantras, love and gratitude practice, awareness, and other practices covered in this book or your own favorite practice.

It is important to note that this discovery is not a fight or resistance of the ego or self; it is actually an invitation of love for ego and self. When you are aware of all your parts and accept, acknowledge and love them, there is no fear or worry that ego is acting. You have invited the ego into the wholeness and oneness that is you and part of "I AM."

Ok, so you made the choice from your heart ... what happens next? Well, get ready, because everything in your life will come to show you and guide you so that you recognize all the barriers, walls, and boundaries that you have created to keep yourself safe and protected. Because those same barriers, walls, and boundaries are the same ones that are keeping you from receiving all that you have wanted: love, acceptance, relationship, and so on. Recognition of self as the I AM takes you beyond the need to and want to, takes you beyond the duality into oneness with everything.

> *Out beyond ideas of wrongdoing and right-doing,*
> *there is a field. I'll meet you there.*
> *When the soul lies down in that grass,*
> *the world is too full to talk about.*
> *Ideas, language, even the phrase 'each other'*
> *doesn't make any sense.*

> — RUMI

I AM is an invitation—an invitation to every part of you to join the whole, for everything outside to join the whole, and to see that everything is just a part of you experiencing you. When you are saying "I AM sad," you are inviting that part of you that is feeling sad into the whole of you. Saying "I AM excited" is you inviting the excited part in the whole.

This is not about stopping emotions or stopping the so-called bad or unwanted from happening. This is a place where you allow all to show up knowing and trusting that it is all a gift. You are inviting the emotion in and breathing through it and allowing it space to move You are not attached to an outcome because the outcome is somewhere out there, and you are standing in the present moment allowing everything to show up spontaneously. You will be releasing your fears that have attached you to expectations or outcomes, and you will no longer be controlling life and rather allowing it to flow with ease and trusting the purpose of it all. Life will give you plenty of opportunities to practice and purge so that you become stronger in your conviction to reach this place of recognition.

At a point that you have deepened your recognition of "I AM" you lose your concerns and controls over choices. When everything shows up as a gift, following your heart and your truth is what feels good. You are not worried so much about mistakes anymore, since every heart-based choice is the right choice. And you are ready receive with open arms all that is showing up in every moment of your life.

The "I AM" is also the recognition that nothing exists outside of you. Meaning that the physical world that you are living in ceases to exist if you were not in this physical form and perceiving it. We are not saying the world stops existing but rather the part of you that is perceiving this world no longer exists. There are other physical forms part of existence and contributing to the creation of the physical world, and you as this physical form are no longer a part of it.

This recognition is important to guide you to the recognition of perception. That you, the self, as part of this physical form is observing the world and experiencing the world through the perception of this physical form, and from that space, you are not and cannot perceive it from the exact view of another physical form. You can empathize and gather information, and it will never be exact. Since to be exact, you have to be totally merged in that other physical form and see it from the eyes, ears, mind, and body of the other.

I can look at a color and say it is green and someone else will look at it and say its green, but I could be seeing the grass green shade while the other person could be seeing forest green. It is still green, but my eyes and the other person's are seeing a slightly different shade. If I hold up a book and each of us is on the opposite side of the book, we can both agree that we are looking at a book however what you are going to describe and what I will describe will be different because you are looking at the front cover and I am looking at the back cover.

This recognition helps you to allow others to have the freedom of their perception and experience while you are free to your perception and experience. The two do not need to match, and both are valid and true. Also, it helps release competition and comparison. Since we are all unique in what we are here to experience and understand. This is an important note in your relationships. To better understand this point, let's look at some examples.

In your relationship, you can ask your partner for assistance, and they have the freedom to say no. Now if you react to what they say then it is on you to seek from your heart and find out why the reaction is present by seeing which part of you asked the question (with what intention/desire for outcome) and why that part is attached to that outcome. Once you become aware of it all then it helps with releasing and letting go of that part. Remember everyone that comes into your life serves a purpose for you to see you. Once you release and let go, your experience shifts as well. This could be in the form that the person is no longer part of your life or that your relationship with them shifts.

Let's look at it all another way. Imagine we are all kids in a playground. You are in the same playground with other kids, and you may prefer to experience the sandbox while someone else prefers the swings. You could both be in the same playground and maybe even on the swing next to each other and one of you could be swinging higher and faster while the other slower and not as high. And this allowing of choice removes right and wrong, good and bad. Everyone is experiencing what feels good to them without judgment, and all are accepted into the playground, free to choose the experience they wish to have.

Now you might say what happens if I am playing in the sandbox with someone and they decide to throw sand at me? This is the other part of what is happening in our worldview, where we are here to heal and release the past for ourselves and those who came before us. In our example, you are grateful for the experience because it is a gift and now you get to practice choice and choosing from your heart. And in doing so, you see your choices of getting angry and walking off, getting angry and throwing sand back, being calm and walking off, getting two other people to come and together throw sand back, or using your voice to ask why the sand was thrown.

When you feel these choices from a heart space rather than a mind and "person/self" space, you are choosing based on love and not fear. And from the place of love, the choice you make will help with the growth and expansion of both you and the other person. And when you choose from heart space and not from a place of hurt, anger and fear and not trying to protect yourself then choices are simple and flowing with ease. You are aware of the hurt, anger and fear and the choice is not to allow that to be your guide but rather love be the guide. Also when you are living life as "I AM" as the self and moving from heart choices then everything comes and happens spontaneously and guided by your intuition and natural flow of life. Actions and choices are not controlled by emotions or thoughts but rather by a natural flow from the heart. Again, emotion and thought can show up, but they are part of the natural flow as well and you are not welling in it.

In the above example, you perceived sand being thrown at you while the other wanted to experience the joy and fun of throwing sand up in the air and seeing what happens. When we are triggered, we are not bothered or triggered by the true intentions but rather our perceived intentions, which are usually attached to a traumatic behavior/pattern from the past. It was not his/her intention for the sand to be thrown at you. From your perception, someone was being mean to you and fear of being hurt kicked in and then anger came to protect, while on the other side, the perception was fun and joy. When you make the heart space choice, the events could turn out to be you being aware of the hurt and fear and anger allowing it space, and for the hurt, fear and anger to be healed and released. You may also choose to say "I did not enjoy the sand being thrown because it got in my hair and eye and I got hurt and I felt sad and angry." On hearing this, the other person may choose to respond, "I am sorry. That was not my intention. I was simply enjoying the sand," in which case you two can go on and play and find a way that you can both enjoy the sandbox if you are both making choices based on heart-space.

At the end of the day, we are little kids (since we still carry our traumatized parts with their stories and behaviors) in a play-ground and each wanting love, attention and playmates, and throwing tantrums and reacting when we have our feelings hurt or feel lonely/alone, unsafe/powerless, and when we don't get what we want.

However, if the other person is not coming from a heart space and is coming from a place of hurt and anger, they could have intentionally thrown the sad because they were feeling ignored and hurt. They could have actually thrown the sand unintentionally but now that you spoke up, they are feeling attacked so now they want to protect themselves so they may throw sand again. You still have a choice to choose from heart space, allow space for you to heal and release the hurt and anger and you may choose to express yourself and walk off.

The more you practice choice and choosing from the heart, and practice awareness, acceptance and love, the more you move with the flow and heart-based choices and actions are naturally flowing and a part of you.

One of my pet peeves used to be people who cut you off in traffic, or the ones that get in the lane that they know is ending only to move up five cars. Especially if they did not wave to thank me. To understand why this was such a big pet peeve, you have to see it from my perspective. I always would do my very best not to cut off people and as soon as I would merge in a lane that I knew was ending, I would merge as soon as I could. This was because it related to a bigger behavior and pattern that I operated under. I wanted to be well-liked and perceived as a good person. I had such a system of checks and balances, of right/wrong, good/bad, fair/unfair. And being liked and good was essential to my survival. Because if I was perceived as good by others then they would like me, would want to be with me, and it would ease the fear of being alone homeless in the street. Because I also had a pattern running that the amount of money I received was attached to how good I am and how much people liked me and want me. So because of what I was carrying in terms of fears and rules anyone that cut me off or would cut me off would drive me crazy as if they are doing it on purpose, "How dare they?" "Why do they get to break the rule?" "What makes them special that they think they can break rules and do what they want?" "What gives them the right to go ahead of all the cars?" You see something seemingly simple for some that they don't even care about had such deep meaning and was so triggering. However, when I let go of my own triggers and released the roots, this was no longer an issue and most time I don't even notice if it is happening. And now without intention I have also found myself cutting off people and even in my own world not realizing the lane was ending. And with that perspective shift, I don't get upset.

The more you are coming from a heart space and love space rather than a mind space and fear space the more your experiences shift to align with the heart and love. Therefore, fewer experiences show up to show you that are carrying fear, anger and hurt since you are now moving away and shifting to more of an unconditional love space. This also means that you are shifting more to seeing and experiencing the world as "I AM."

A question that often arises in terms of relationships, especially as partners, lovers, husband/wife, and family, is "Then what is the point of a relationship if it is not to support each other, love each other, be there for each other, do things for each other."

The only point of a relationship with anyone, even an interaction with a total stranger, is simply for them to be a mirror for you to see yourself and recognize the "I AM." And I know some of you reading this right now are saying "Isn't that being selfish?" and the answer is no. First of all, when you are coming from a place of unconditional love and acceptance then selfishness ceases to exist. Because when you love and accept yourself unconditionally, you love and accept others unconditionally as well, and you allow yourself and others to be free. When you are asking these questions, you are coming from a fear-based mind that is demanding out of fear of being alone and not being loved. But when you are coming from a love-based heart then you are receiving love and support from so many different sources. This removes the need for a single person or group of people to provide for all your needs to fill the holes that your fears and mind has created inside. From the love-based heart, you are whole and complete and there is nothing needed to fill you up, and relationships become about ease, freedom, flow, dance and love.

Recognition and discovering "I AM" allows you to see the I AM in the other, in the experience itself, in the one experiencing and as an observer of it all. You are the teacher, the student, the lesson/knowledge, the classroom, and the school. You are the lover the beloved, the love exchanged between the two and observing it all. In recognizing and discovering "I AM" then you discover that there is nothing outside of you. The more we let go of fear and align with our heart and love, the more we are aligned with "I AM" and we shift to a space of allowing all to show up spontaneously and since nothing is outside of us then there is nothing to fear. And even fear loses its meaning and becomes part of the whole, and it is not triggering. In this space, there is a natural gratitude that arises in your heart and your being.

This is not something anyone can teach you; it is a place that you can be guided to. And this book is providing a way and guidance to this discovery. There are many roads and many ways to get here and there are many people that will come and guide you along the way. The key is that you choose from the heart to walk and along the way allow your heart to be your guide. And you are always being guided in many different ways and forms, and the Universe (you to you) is always communicating via repeating numbers, songs, movies, road signs. It also communicates through nature, when we receive messages from trees, flowers, birds, animals, wind and so much more. Be open to receiving the messages and don't brush them off as "it is in my head" or "it's a coincidence." How else is the unseen world supposed to communicate with you? How else are you going to receive the guidance and clues?

When you discover this place, life becomes about living and the experience of living. It becomes about the flow and flowing. The judgments disappear, fear disappears, the rule book disappears, and attachments disappear. Love and gratitude become part of experiences.

As nice as all this sounds, fear takes over when you set on this path. The fear of how will I live, what will life be like, how are things going to be … You have worked hard in your life trying to fit it, following the rule books, controlling life and situations, have your badges of being good, nice, spiritual, smart, successful, talented, hard worker, good friend, kind, etc and now you are being asked to let go of all those badges, letting go of control and the rule books. So it is a natural response for fear to come and say NO. Fear is saying I know this place, I know the dark spots and shadows, I know how to hide and I know when to move, I know I have money and can make money with my job, I know some people like me and some love me and some look up to me, I am part of society and now you want me to give it all up and trust and go with the flow? I don't think so.

Another big fear is the fear of loss, which is the main fear. One of the forms of this fear of loss is saying I know how to be in the shadows and be in this life with its struggles and suffering, I know how to manage my sadness and disappointments, but if I move out of this place into a place that everything is good and working out and then you come and take the stuff away or something happens then I won't be able to recover. In other words, I know how to move in shit and be in shit but if you take me out and give me good stuff, I know at some point the other shoe is going to drop (because it always does) but then I am too used to the good stuff and won't know how to manage the loss or what to do. No thanks. Fear of having and then losing is much more than fear of not having, not receiving because how can you lose something you don't have or have not received?

You are used to wanting to receive and OK with not receiving; you are used to that longing. But then to receive it and then lose it, that is a loss hard to recover from. So you dance around what you want to receive and are perfectly OK with not fully receiving it. Awareness and trust practice helps and moving into a place where having something delicious even for one second is worth it.

Another way to recognize and move into this realization of "I AM" is the flower of life and sacred geometry.

Everything is connected and there is an overlay. There is also one outer form that encompasses the whole, and there is a space outside the whole as well (one observing the whole). Now bring that knowledge into your existence and see that we are all connected to the source, there is a single source, and in each of us in this form is a single source (heart). There is a connection and overlay to everyone, everything, in the seen and unseen. And the whole and complete includes all. You are the seeker, the finder, the object/knowledge, and the observer of it all. Or better yet, *You* are the victim, the abuser, the pain, the love, the forgiveness, and the one observing all of it. And even better, you are the giver, the receiver, the gift, and the one who created it all.

You don't need to work hard. There is no finish line to get to. It is just a deepening the recognition of "I AM." Everyone in this physical form is on the same path of recognizing and deepening this recognition, even the gurus and masters. I am a master and humbled student at the same time.

We are all explorers on this journey helping each other home, which is the grace and love inside our heart.

I leave you with a favorite poem to get you started; The Guest House by Jalaluddin Rumi, Translated by Coleman Barks:

> *This being human is a guest house.*
> *Every morning a new arrival.*
> *A joy, a depression, a meanness,*
> *some momentary awareness comes*
> *as an unexpected visitor.*
> *Welcome and entertain them all!*
> *Even if they're a crowd of sorrows,*
> *who violently sweep your house*
> *empty of its furniture,*
> *still, treat each guest honorably.*
> *He may be clearing you out*
> *for some new delight.*
> *The dark thought, the shame, the malice,*
> *meet them at the door laughing,*
> *and invite them in.*
> *Be grateful for whoever comes,*
> *because each has been sent*
> *as a guide from beyond.*

10

THE BODY

This brings us to our home: our bodies. The body is amazing at healing and releasing naturally. Over the years, the program responses have changed from the original program. Good news is that you can reset it. But we must get out of the way.

How do you do that? By trusting yourself, your heart and your body. The trust allows you let go of control, listen and allow. Your task becomes to only witness and allow. The body does the rest.

Remember the list of my ailments from earlier in this book? Also consider that I came from a family line with heart attacks, high blood pressure, high cholesterol, and some cancer. I am fifty-one, and I am in the best physical shape of my life. I do not have physical issues; I do not take medication for any illness, just some supplements that my body has asked for (moringa, collagen, calcium, etc.). My skin looks better than ten years ago. I run better than when I was in my thirties. I eat what my body tells me to and when it needs it. And I eat everything and enjoy my food. I exercise when my body wants and do what it is asking for that day. And when it wants rest, I make sure it gets the rest needed. I love my life, myself and my body. I don't have a job or career, rather I am following my passion, and that is to be of service. Every day I see the abundance flowing to me in many shapes and forms. And in every moment, I am amazed by this magical magnificent life and this extraordinary home, my body.

All the trauma, emotions and generational baggage is stored in the body. Even when we release and heal emotionally and energetically, the memory of it needs to be cleared by the body.

Look at it as a computer. Your computer has a cache where it stores data. The computer stores data in the cache memory for fastest access to memory locations. But the cache needs to be cleared of any unused and unnecessary data from time to time.

Your body is holding on to the data about past experiences in the muscles, bones, and nerves. The body needs to be cleared of this unnecessary data for the body, mind, and heart to be aligned and function in harmony. The more aligned and in harmony you are with the heart, the more you move from a love/heart space.

When you trust and love your body, it means you listen to the body—when it wants to eat, what it wants to eat, when to exercise, what exercise to do, and so much more. You don't eat your food when you are "supposed to eat" but when the body tells you it's hungry. You don't eat just any food but rather what your body is asking for. You don't go to the gym because you have to but because your body is asking for it.

Also let go of your rules and judgments about exercise and food. There are no rules. The only rule is to listen and connect to your body. Let go of your judgements about different foods. Let go of your judgements about your body and age. Finally, let go of judgements how your body is supposed to move and what it's supposed to do.

If you are at a weight that you know your body is not happy with then know that there is a purpose that you put that weight onto the body. People with long standing generation trauma and/or history of trauma in their lives tend to have weight issues. They may sometimes even have eating disorders. The weight we put on the body is because the body feels it needs protection from the outside. When we stress the body, be it due to emotions, excessive exercise, denying nutrients, doing what we hate, or stress of life, then the body is receiving a signal that something is wrong, prepare the body and hold on to whatever you can to protect the body. When the stressors are gone, the connection to the body is back to what it needs to be, then you will start to see the body coming to its ideal weight and health.

Make peace with food. If every time you have ice cream and you feel bad, telling yourself you should not be eating it, and that is bad for you, either don't eat it, let go of judgement and then eat it or take time to get in a better place right before you eat it. This is because it's not the ice cream that is making you fat, it's the thoughts and energy that you are consuming while eating it. If you have judgments about certain foods "harming your body," then remove the judgement or get in a better place before eating it.

When I have a craving for cookies, I know my body is trying to get my attention that my sugar is low and it needs sugar, so I choose honey or a date. When my body is asking for red meat specifically, I know my iron is low. When my body is asking for peanut butter, I know my body wants protein.

I used to run and exercise to relieve stress. And since I started to shift my way of life, now the type of exercise, duration and amount is dictated by my body.

And when the programing of the body is functioning properly, our emotions are no longer feared or looked at with a label of good and bad. This body becomes the guesthouse, where emotions can be invited in. They will not have any weight; they will come in and leave. Remember, inviting means we are not separating and therefore loving each guest that visits.

You can say I am afraid or I am sad, but it would be just as if you are saying there is a door or a window. And this happens because you are no longer attached to the emotions via the weight of the past stories.

An important part of connecting with your body is balancing it. Our bodies, regardless of gender, have both the masculine and feminine side (right and left sides respectively). Understanding that each and every one of us carries both energies; which energy has been the dominant one that we have used in our life; forgiving and asking forgiveness of both parts; allowing each to be present and function as it needs to; and lastly bringing them together and balancing them.

The feminine side of our bodies—left side—is connected to the energy of love, receiving, nurturing, nourishing, and protecting (as in womb, mother-child). The masculine side of our bodies—right side—is connected to more giving, letting go, and being a provider and protector/warrior. Life and generational traumas have caused these imbalances in both genders.

If you want balance in your life and want a balance between receiving and giving, your feminine and masculine sides need to be balanced.

If we are to bring balance to our world, we must balance these energies in ourselves. Many women have hidden or buried their feminine side for survival reasons, therefore their masculine side is more dominant. This is so that they are not labeled too emotional or weak. With majority of men and women giving more weight to their masculine energies, the world we live in has lost its balance. So regardless of gender, or sexual preference, each and every one of us must bring balance back in our bodies to shift and balance our world.

There are various techniques for clearing the memory data from the body some of which are, Energy Healing, Emotional Code, Body Code, Tapping, Acupuncture, Yoga, Pilates, Stretching. I have also put together a masterclass combining the healing services with releasing the memory from the body. Whatever you choose, choose based on what feels good for you and your body. And you can do a combination of services as well.

It is important that with any method you choose you still listen to your body and trust it. If you are doing yoga, don't go based on the instructors or other students' tempo. Move with your own breath and stay in a position if it feels good to you.

Let your heart and body be your guide. They will not lead you stray. Trust. Love.

11
TAKE AWAY

Some of the important take aways from the book:

Set your intention to merge with your heart.

Do not be afraid to make mistakes, because everything falls into place when you follow your heart. Keep trusting.

Connect with nature in any way you can. Let nature be your guide. It's the best teacher you will have.

At the end of all the triggers, there is fear, so let go of your fears and keep reminding yourself that "I am safe, I am loved, I am supported" … let this be your mantra throughout the day.

You always have choice.

Practice awareness as much as you can throughout the day … let the natural observer in you be the main part of your day.

Let go of control, to receive all that you want in life. Because your fears, are making you to control life. The control is not keeping you safe, it is just keeping you from being able to flow with life.

Be open to receiving and seeing the magic around you. There is so much if you are just open and willing to see and receive and not let your mind tell you it's in your head, it's a coincidence. Even if it is, if it is bringing you joy, does it even really matter? I see hearts all the time. And some may argue about some of what I see as a heart not to be a heart. It does not matter, because for me seeing hearts is a feeling inside and a communication I have with my heart and outside world. It reminds me of my purpose and that I am on the right path.

Every day is an opportunity for a new beginning, so treat it as a restart or reset, and practice gratitude and love for all of it as much as you can in the day.

Change your perspective, look at every situation that is presented in your life as universe helping you. Life is always helping you and not against you.

Let go of your rule book and measuring scale and be willing to see and put more value on the good stuff. Sitting in traffic, spilling coffee as you are about to go out, tripping and stubbing your toe, and waking up with a headache should not be measurements of having a bad day. Even with these moments, there is so much happening that you could shift your day to appreciation and gratitude if you were willing to see.

It is ok for things to fall apart or end, because it is an opportunity to build something new or start something new. As kids when you played with blocks you build something and then took it down and build something new. Creating is about expanding on what is there or doing something new. When you are designing something, you are going to have a first version and then keep improving it until you come up with something final. Even that the final version after awhile you will find other ways to enhance it.

We each have our own beauty and perfume. We each can enhance this world with our individual expressions of how we live our lives.

Loving life and enjoying life is possible and doable and it is independent of what is happening around you or in the world.

The change that you want on the outside and in the world can only happen from the inside of you.

PRACTICE EXERCISES

TAKE RESPONSIBILITY

When you wake up every morning, remind yourself that you are responsible for your life by stating: "I take full responsibility for my life and my choices. I am the creator of my life."

Also, if you become aware that you are blaming others or a situation or life or God throughout the day, repeat the affirmation several times or until the emotions are more relaxed.

When speaking to others, speak from "I" place, meaning I want … I need … I see … I like … from my perspective … this way you are taking responsibility for yourself and your emotions and letting others take responsibility for theirs. And remember both perspectives can be valid and true.

AWARENESS - MINDFULNESS PRACTICES

It's a good time to point out that the original intention of meditation was mindfulness before modern society changed meditation to rest and relaxation and quieting the mind. Mindfulness is the art of not following the stories and the noise of the mind and staying present for whatever is showing up at the moment.

Start and end your day with Gratitude: I know you have heard this a million times and you might even respond that you are so grateful for your life and all that you have. However, this gratitude is a bit different since in some ways you are doing your gratitude routine with your mind rather than your heart. And by that, I mean it has become a task and full of fear and anxiety and your mind is in charge of what you should say you are grateful for rather than your heart. To bring heart back into it, we must bring love and fun back into it.

Before you get out of bed as you first are about to open your eyes, feel your pillow, your mattress, your bed, and become aware of all the wonderful gadgets that you have to keep track of your sleep or help you sleep better, breathe better, and wake you up. Now send some love and gratitude to your pillow, mattress, bed, sheets, and each gadget. For example, "I love my pillow—thank you for being so comfortable to my neck. I love my sheets—thank you for being so cozy and comfortable. I love my phone—thank you, I don't even know what I would do without you… etc." Be creative, there are so many things that you can love and be grateful for other than your home, job, money in the accounts and your loved ones. Gratitude for the window that lets in the sun every morning. Gratitude for the roof that keeps the home safe from the weather. Gratitude for the nighttime and darkness that reminded the body it was time to have a deep rest and allowed for it to happen. Finish your morning gratitude with "I am reborn each morning into a brand new me and a brand-new day. I am grateful for this brand-new day that is full of amazing possibilities and magic."

Daily routine life practice: There are so many routines that we have each day, and we go through them mindlessly like machines, pretty checked out. Those are the best ones to be mindful of since that is the time that the mind is activated, and the thoughts are constantly flowing. Here are some sample daily routines and how to bring mindfulness to them:

Showering: gratitude for your clean water and shower, gratitude for water itself for cleansing, and feeling the suds and hands and the body as you are washing yourself. Also, you can feel that the water and shampoo/soap are cleaning more than just dirt, they also are removing layers that no longer serve you.

Cooking: gratitude not just for the bounty of all the ingredients you are using but also all the effort that has taken to bring you the ingredient, from the elements in nature to farmer, delivery, grocers, and more. Also, take time to bring gratitude to the animal and produce for their sacrifice to bring your body the nutrients that your body needs. Then as you are cooking and tasting mindfulness as you are cleaning, cutting, or stirring, feeling your connection as if you are performing a dance.

Eating: gratitude portion just as above and mindfulness to distinguish the ingredients used, the flavors, the consistency in your mouth and how the food is traveling in your body to your stomach.

Drinking: bringing gratitude for what you have and being mindful as you open or prepare your drink, pouring it into the glass and with each sip feeling the drink in your mouth as it travels through your body.

So, the above practices are good to connect you back to your body and bring you to the present moment. Doing them more and more brings more peace and joy to your day to your life. Also, it helps to move your energy in a way to release the toxic energies that you have been carrying that no longer align with your true self. But how do awareness and mindfulness work when we are not doing an active activity and are being triggered with our personas? Best way to go inside and keep pointing back to yourself and going deeper.

What do awareness and mindfulness look like as you are going through your day, having conversations, doing your work, getting ready for meetings, etc.? At this point, just being a neutral observer to your life, stepping outside of yourself and watching your reactions, interactions, emotions, thoughts, and behaviors. No touching it, not judging it, just a curious observer taking unbiased notes as to what is happening. Sort of like the courtroom stenographers that are just typing what is being said—they are not formulating an opinion about anything; they are just taking notes. So is your observer—he/she is just observing any emotion that comes up without labeling it good or bad, observing any actions without judgment of it being good or bad, and any thoughts that are coming up allow them to bubble up without having them get connected. Easy? Yes and no. If you are not being triggered and able to stay neutral to it all then yes, it is easy but what happens for most people is that they get triggered by an emotion or thought or something that is happening outside and connects them to a learned pattern and behavior. Sometimes even one pattern and behavior sets in motion several other programs as well.

When you are triggered, it's the same method of observing as a neutral bystander but with a twist. If you are continuously doing the mindfulness and awareness daily exercises as mentioned earlier in this chapter, you can rest assured that at some point your observer is going to kick in and take notice of your emotions, thoughts, and actions.

And when your observer takes notice, depending on the severity/intensity of the trigger, you may practice any of the following:

- Continue to be a neutral observer and allow emotions, thoughts, and actions to rise and fall by themselves without any participation or interaction. This exercise is much easier if the trigger is not very severe. The best way to be a neutral observer is to stay in awareness and not get involved in the story of the part of you that is experiencing all the emotions and thoughts.
- If the severity of the trigger is such that it is very intense and/or there are multiple triggers, which makes it difficult to be neutral, then allow the emotions and thoughts to come out on a piece of paper. This is different from journaling. You are still staying in a place of neutrality and just letting it all come out on a single piece of paper without getting

involved. You can keep writing over on this paper until all that is needed to be said comes out then burn the paper in a secure place before releasing the ashes in nature.

PRACTICING CHOICE

From the moment you are about to wake up in bed until you get in bed and close your eyes, you have choices. Always remind yourself. As you are in bed, there is a moment when you are awake but not really awake to move or get up. That is the point to remind yourself you have choices. And don't worry if you missed it; just catch the next moment to see choices. The point of this exercise is that as much as you can throughout the day give yourself choices and choose from your heart. Always have at least three choices especially at the beginning. Yes or no choices work as well; however, stay away from yes or no and try to have three or more choices at the beginning. It's important to see you have many choices at the beginning and practice finding what feels best.

Before you get up, you can see what your choices are. Choice A: get up right away and get started on your day. Choice B: stay in bed for another ten minutes. Choice C: get up, have coffee, and relax then get started. With each choice, either imagine the choice in a box or that you are holding the choice in your hands and bringing it to your heart center and just feeling the choice. You will notice a small difference in the feeling of each one and one will feel better than the rest. So that is the choice for you from your heart. And if you see that is the choice that is asking to stay in bed for 10 min and then anxiety takes over, then see from the remaining choices what feels best and choose that. With this practice, you are choosing either what feels best from your heart space or what feels easiest in that moment from your heart space, which may be different from what feels BEST.

PRACTICE LOVE AND GRATITUDE

In the awareness and mindfulness practice section, I have already listed some of the love and gratitude practices.

As you are lying in bed, still half asleep and not ready to get out of bed, just feel in that moment what are you grateful for? A good night's sleep, your pillow, your blanket, your sheets, your mattress, your bed, the window next to your bed, your phone, your PJs, or your skin if you are sleeping naked, your partner next to you...? And whatever in that moment is bringing you joy, and you are grateful for then say (either out loud or to yourself) "I love my pillow—thank you, my pillow, for supporting my head" and continue for all the things that are bringing you joy.

Then spend some time bringing love and gratitude to yourself and your body. Take five external body parts within your sight and five body internal body parts and bring love and gratitude to each one. The key is that you must really love this body part and not just fake it. And if you cannot find five then do as many as you can until you get to find more. For example:

Examples of expressing love and gratitude to yourself and your body would be saying "I love my eyes—thank you for letting me see this beautiful colorful world. I love my eyelashes—thank you for keeping things out of my eyes and protecting my eyes. I love my skin—thank you for protecting my body so well. I love my arms—thank you for letting me hug the people I love. I love my hair—thank you for protecting my scalp and making me look beautiful. I love my lungs—thank you for the breath that I take in each moment. I love my spleen—not sure what your function is but I love you and I am grateful for you for doing your part in my body. I love my blood—thank you for all that you do for my body. Without you, this body could not work. I love my joints—thank you for helping this body move. I love my heart—thank you for beating strong, taking care of this body and helping me love.

PRACTICES TO HELP RECOGNIZE I AM

A. Please note, do this practice only if you do not have a fear of the ocean, water, or swimming. And if it brings any anxiety, stop and just focus on your breath. Read the poem below and then lie down. Imagine you are floating on top of the water, and there are no other species inside the water (so no sharks, stingrays, fishes etc.). You are seeing and interacting with all that you are seeing and hearing and could have reactions of fear, anxiety, frustration, and even peace. Then imagine you are comfortable and have the means to breathe underwater and slowly float down a couple of feet below the surface of the water and you are facing the sky. Feel that your body is lighter, the noises are muffled and you cannot make out the clouds too much; just the light coming through. After a few breaths, float a couple of feet down and feel that you are even lighter and it's less noisy, and you are just now only seeing the light. Continue to float down, pausing every couple of feet to notice that you are lighter, with less noise and the light breaking through the water and shining down until you reach the bottom. By the time you are all the way down, you should be feeling the peace and that you let go of all the noise inside and outside and just light and floating and feeling the light.

Deep underwater, Looking up
The waves of the ocean pass
The clouds in the sky pass
The storm too will pass

Deep underwater, Looking up
The noise gets quiet
The movement gets slow
The light always shines

Deep underwater, Looking up
I am the 'Ocean'
I am the 'Sky'
I am at Peace

Deep underwater, Looking up
Light fills my heart
I am grateful
I AM ...

— ATOUSA RAISSYAN

B. This is better if done outside and barefoot on the grass or dirt but can be done anywhere. Stand and just feel the body bring your attention to your heartbeat. Be reminded that the heart is beating on its own and naturally without any effort and any doing by you. Just feel the heartbeat for a few moments. YOU are just the observer of the heartbeat. Then bring your attention to the lungs and breath. Feel how the lungs and diaphragm are functioning naturally and the breath flowing naturally, without any involvement from you. YOU are just the observer of the breath and body. Feel the breath for a few moments. Then start to walk slowly and notice the body is moving naturally—there is no doing. You are not telling your arms, feet, or body how to move all is happening naturally and YOU are just observing this movement. Then as you are moving observe that the seeing is happening naturally without any effort or doing and YOU are just observing what is being seen by the eyes. Continue this process and notice that whatever arises, even thoughts or emotions, just naturally arises just like the heartbeat and the breath and you are just observing it all.

13
CLIENT STORIES

TAMMY'S STORY

I began working with healers fourteen years ago when I wanted to facilitate a career change which meant going to graduate school. You see I tried graduate school once before which did not work out. However, I knew this time was different because I had kept that dream to myself. Also, I wanted a more stable career going into my forties. However, I was not completely sure how to start making that connection.

Fortunately, I had a friend who was already doing a lot of healing with a somatic healer. I was seeking my own transformation so I asked for his contact information. I reached out and we agreed to start working together about six months before I started graduate school. My first healing experience transformed the top layers to achieve my goal. I felt euphoric and excited to start the next chapter of my life across the country in my new career field.

Unfortunately, my euphoric feelings dwindled quickly. My new work environment immediately triggered me. During that time period, the word trigger was not even in my vocabulary so I was not able to ground myself. Within a year I started experiencing some weird health issues which led to diagnostic testing. In the end, the test results were either negative or inconclusive. I knew I was not the same person though it seemed like nothing had changed since I was trying to hold on.

A couple of years later, I found myself at another crossroads. I connected with the same friend who had moved onto a new healer. I was intrigued. During a short road trip, I learned more about her experience. Her new healer specialized in depth hypnosis and shamanic healing. She talked about soul retrieval and spirit guides which completely resonated. She recommended that I see a different healer who worked in the same practice. I wrote to the shamanic healer about my journey. We agreed to work together and set a date and time for our first appointment. In between setting the appointment, I broke my ankle which was surgically repaired. I laid in bed wondering where is my life going and what is happening. I recall thinking to myself. Will this ever get better? What is wrong with me?

During my second healing experience, I committed over two years of my life on transforming my trauma. I met my first spirit guide who is a starfish. I am grateful for that period of my life which was filled with a range of emotions. I learned about triggers and answered questions which I had tortured my for years.

My work took every ounce of my energy. I found myself mostly by myself though I did not feel alone. I took myself out to reconnect to places and events I loved which I craved. I regained power that I had lost over my lifetime. Eventually, I outgrew my second healer as new relationships and work came into my life. I was definitely in a better place and felt like my healing took root. As life moved along, the next junction showed up.

Once again, I found myself triggered, which I did not see immediately until it was pointed out. When I did see it, I knew my personal and professional relationships were suffering. I had given away my power and was determined to reconnect it. Shortly after I acknowledged my state of mind, I started searching for my new healer. I had a very clear vision of what I needed for the next part

of my healing journey. I knew I wanted to work with a shaman in-person since my last healer with virtual.

I began my search last June where I was pleasantly surprised to see a handful of practitioners in my area who could potentially meet my criteria. The first shaman I researched was actually moving her practice out of state. I thought deal breaker since I knew I wanted to meet in person. As I sifted through my search results, I found Atousa.

I started browsing her website where I felt drawn into prose and photos. I found her offerings intriguing so I decided to browse her socials. During my socials research, I found her podcast Goodbye Bull****, Hello Happiness. I stumbled upon Episode 37: Understanding your triggers and how to help yourself. I hung on every word of that podcast and thought this is it.

I decided to write Atousa about my journey and inquire about working together. She replied and happily agreed to a brief call which sealed the deal. Atousa has been a constant in my life since I started working with her. Last year I spent most of my Friday afternoons with Atousa healing my inner child wounds in her sanctuary.

I knew my unresolved trauma and triggers were blocking me from living an authentic life which meant speaking freely, feeling grounded, and trusting my heart. I truly believe I was guided to her when I had the emotional capacity, time, and focus to fully engage in this incredibly transformative work.

Although, I had worked other healers before who used similar modalities, they were nothing like Atousa. After a handful of sessions, I felt her humanity while chanting a mantra she had given me during my morning practice. My process was an incredibly transformative journey that shifted and lightened me in ways I could not have imagined.

My soul released burdens that were never mine to carry, I got to see myself from the inside out, and let down some sturdy walls that protected my heart. I twisted, turned, and blocked at times because it was scary to feel so vulnerable though in same breath you are loved, guided, and held in an incredible amount of space that frees you from your pain and fears.

I healed the wounds and merged the shadows to fully illumi-nate the light inside me that eternally shines!

I learned that I have always been on my journey and the roads that led me to Atousa all had purpose. I learned to see, trust, love, and give voice to myself. Atousa tells you that things come in layers and that is how they get released which is a process. I can share the process cannot be rushed and in reflection you want to go together because there is so much goodness and "magic" that you will want to experience all of it.

Atousa's an extraordinary human being who is an incredible healer. She makes the world a more peaceful place simply by existing. Although I felt like a stranger when I first started seeing Atousa, I left with an unexpected gift of friendship.

Tammy.

CHELSEA'S STORY

Before stumbling across Atousa on Google, I was a money-motivated sales professional. My career defined me. My addiction to work started when I was a young girl. I started working (by choice) in elementary school. I believe my first job was assisting a friend and her mom in delivering the local Gazette once a week. Growing up, I got straight As, played sports, and always worked in various capacities—school admin, special education assistant, retailer, hostess, waitress, lifeguard, lifeguard manager, National Cancer Institute intern, and then I was onto college.

Determined to become a pediatric oncologist after my internship, I quickly realized a biology major wasn't for me. I didn't connect with any of my professors, and I was no longer lit up by what I was studying. It wasn't until later in life that I realized it didn't work out. But, determined to graduate to prove to the world that I was capable, I quickly switched to a communications major with a concentration in public relations. I got an internship at a local college, from a patron I waited on at an Italian spot where I was waiting tables. I did the work and graduated in four years. Like my childhood, I worked my way through college finding my entrepreneurial bug and finding fun, random, short-term jobs. This afforded me the opportunity to have a lot of fun in college and do whatever I wanted. This is why I ultimately made a career out of sales—financial freedom with no ceiling on my earnings.

I was conditioned by society and lost who I was at my core. I became materialistic and my past traumas manifested into too many mysterious health problems in my twenties. It was sometime around my early thirties when I started to question the purpose of my life. I surpassed all of my dreams—I got the cars, a beautiful home, the title, the promotions, the salary, and the commissions. I was on top, but I felt empty inside and unfulfilled. I spent tens of thousands of dollars on the best holistic services, every type of therapy imaginable (hypnosis, CBT, DBT, EMDR, etc.), and nothing changed. I questioned if I was clinically depressed. As it turns out, I needed deeper healing from being too good at stuffing down trauma and microtraumas. Being a good girl, a rule follower, and an achiever takes a toll on you that manifests later in life as a perfectionist, people pleaser, and someone with no boundaries.

Enter Atousa. As always, I go big or go home. I wanted instant gratification to rid me of all my problems. I knocked on the door of this stranger, Atousa's house, took off my shoes and lay on a masseuse table waiting to try Reiki for the first time. Reviews claimed Atousa was the therapist for therapists and their patients they couldn't treat. I heard strange noises coming from Atousa and was thinking what did I get myself into? Then it was on to sound bowls and crystals. I knew one day I'd be writing about my experience, but that was just the beginning. I decided to take Atousa's guidance to do a life transformation. I would meet with Atousa weekly/biweekly to heal the little girl within me. But this was no traditional unpacking like at talk therapy. It was speaking to the little girl within me convincing her she was safe and loved. Atousa saw all the trauma I was holding in and refused to use fearmongering to tell me what she saw me go through (when I couldn't remember or recall because trauma will do that to you).

We worked through all the ages, and some weeks I felt like I was on cloud nine and other weeks I would sleep all day or physically vomit or find myself screaming at the top of my lungs out of the blue. My body was purging itself of the person I've become and all the conditioning of right and wrong. At the end of the rainbow, there was a beautiful woman full of joy and unconditional love who was ready to take on the world. She landed multiple new jobs where she was focused on having fun more than the pay. She cared less about what people think and just lived her best life. She became a great listener, communicator, and healer, and lived a life full of abundance. Her medical mysteries would subside until it was time to do the work again (yes, it's a process and we are never done).

I started my journey to self-love with Atousa on February 27, 2021, and I count my lucky stars to this date for stumbling upon the best teacher and mentor to enter my life through divine connection. Nearly two years since Atousa graduated me, she has remained a great friend and mentor, always checking in and expecting nothing in return. The tools she gave me are rock solid as I haven't had to book a maintenance appointment with her because I hold the power within me to live the life of my dreams. I wake up every single day with immense gratitude for the woman I've become and continue my daily affirmations and EFT.

I was tested recently when I was laid off from a job I loved. I was promoted numerous times and built the team of my dreams that was grounded in love, mutual respect, and fun. But rather than feel sorry for myself, I knew when one door closes another one opens. There were a few bad days, but I consistently used the tools Atousa taught me. I also listened to my intuition, which told me to take a break from work to recharge for the next exciting opportunity. I knew a voice would tell me when it was time. I spent my time unemployed ensuring my team landed on their feet giving them career guidance that would allow them to land a job in a role with a great culture and coaching them to not settle for less than they deserve. As fate would have it, my girls as I would call them landed jobs quickly making much more money than I was able to pay them. That was so important for me as I've never had a boss do this for me. After nearly two months of unemployment, I was more confident and energized than ever that I was getting called to my next adventure. And, for the first time in my adult life, I asked for help! I used the power of LinkedIn and had an unprecedented number of people ready to hire me allowing me to interview companies and have my pick on what I wanted the next chapter of my career life to look like.

Atousa allowed me to discover my purpose in life: to help others become their best self via unconditional love. It turns out I wasn't meant to become a pediatric oncologist because I was called to transform the business world and shape future business leaders. Contrary to popular belief, unconditional love and happiness belong in the workplace. We spend roughly 33% of our lives working, and humans deserve to be their authentic selves in a safe environment without fear of retaliation.

This doesn't even scratch the surface of the reasons why I'm thankful for Atousa, but I hope it inspires you. You can receive it all and you deserve it all, whatever that means to you. Thank you, Atousa, for allowing me to not only see a world full of pure love and goodness but most importantly see it win me and others. I no longer reject love, but I. Am. Love!

Chelsea Bass

SARA'S STORY

Atousa asked me to write about my experience working with her. I chose to write a letter to my past self, just before I meet her. And here is that letter:

Dear Sara,

I am writing to tell you that immense joy and happiness is possible... I know you have felt misunderstood all of your life. Being adopted left you feeling worthless, and your emotionally immature parents wanted you, but didn't know how to show love in a healthy way. Your dad was angry and explosive, sometimes violent. Your mom was the opposite and held in and ate her anger and fears. As someone who feels every emotion deeply, but is surrounded by others who do not, and being shamed for your feelings leaves you confused, angry and deeply sad.

You inherited all the societal and generational baggage that we all do, and did not understand that it wasn't yours to carry. So you twisted you thoughts, actions and body to match the energies and life patterns around you, even though it didn't make any sense to your heart. You swallowed your confusion, anger, sadness, and all the other big emotions, and put on a strong front.

I know you think you're dying right now. Your body isn't working because you have a hateful relationship with it. You were never taught a body was an amazing gift. You were taught it is like a naughty child, misbehaving and inconvenient. So that is why you struggle to walk more than 10 feet.

That is why you can barely get up stairs, and you can't stand for more than a couple minutes before you lower back and knees cry out in agony, forcing you to sit or lay down. And at 43, this is embarrassing to you. You feel weak, helpless.

But, wait, you quit a massive drug addiction suddenly and on your own. You should feel proud, but all you feel is secret and complete shame. Even though that experience was needed to understand the nature of addiction, depression, anxiety, and suicidal thoughts so that in the future, you can use that information to help others.

You have PTSD from years on caring for your Mother-in-Law, who felt more like a mom in that moment than your mom. From seeing Death up close, literally seeing him dance, and deep confusion and fear about the orbs and fairies and other energies that you started feeling/hearing/seeing the last few years of her life.

You tried everything you could—you were desperate. You went to a Mental Health Crisis Center afraid you had schizophrenia, but they said you were fine. I know you felt broken and scared and pissed that no one seemed to want to help you.

Traditional Cognitive Behavioral therapy provided a tiny glimpse of hope, but the process was painfully slow, and you can feel something was missing. But you don't know what. Luckily, your therapist will suggest to follow the spiritual thread as it isn't something she can help with.

Soon, you will meet Atousa. And your entire life will change. From Jan to June 2022 you will work on your mental health with her. You will learn how to heal yourself from the inside out. Everything we need is inside of us, and we get to choose what we are ready to do or not do.

And Atousa will help you to be brave enough to let your light shine, and share it with others without fear. You will discover inner peace. You will find an entire pantheon of energies/entities/spirits that have always been there, have been trying to help, but your fear colored glasses made them appear scary and tormenting.

You will love more freely, and learn to appreciate the villains as well as the heroes in your life. Being a music teacher will become even more rewarding than before, because you won't hold back sharing your soul with your students. And that will help them share theirs with others.

Your mother will die, and you will not only be there to comfort her, but the fear you had with your Mother-in-law will be healed and you will see the beautiful gift of being with someone for their last breath. You will cry sad/happy tears because you love her so much, but your grief won't trap you for years like it did before. Because you see a bigger picture.

You know now how things work in YOUR WORLD. And that is the biggest gift Ms. Atousa will give us. She will help us understand ourselves, the magic around us, how to allow life to flow in all of it's wonderous directions. From there, we create our own life. And as my ancestors reminded me recently, We are ALWAYS never alone.

Hang on Sara, help is nearly there.
Love, Sara

DAISY'S STORY

Working with Atousa has been transformative.

I still remember navigating through her website and reading online reviews about her services while trying to figure out if I really wanted to give this approach a try or not. And what is a shaman anyways? Back then, I was not entirely sure what to expect from working with a shaman, and I didn't know much about how the process works - I only had some ideas from self-help books written by other shamans. I had so many questions, doubts, and worries in mind, but these were minor when compared to an unshakable feeling of being stuck and directionless overall. On the outside, this was not obvious, I seemed fine, pretty much normal.

A that point in my life, I had already obtained a graduate degree, a job, and many of the expected accomplishments for a young adult. I am used to be goal driven and typically achieve what I set myself out to do. Yet, I didn't feel like anything was good enough and, somehow, was struggling with communicating with others effectively, as if a part of me had closed out from others. And so, one day I said to myself: "giving this a try will either do nothing, and just be a waste of time and money, or it will actually do something like what others described in their reviews".

In either case, I wouldn't know if or how this was going to work for me if I didn't try and I was running out of ideas on what to do next, so I booked a session with Atousa just to see what this was all about. It helped that Atousa has a straight-forward process that lets you choose a goal and work towards it; I chose to work on improving my communication skills as I felt as if I had lost my voice. I wanted to better connect with others.

All set and ready for my first session, I stepped into her studio with no expectations of whether this would have any real impact in my life, nor with any definite plans about making this a long-term commitment. But one session with Atousa was all it took for me to decide this was worth a try, and I was worth the effort. Unknowingly, I had surrendered to my process of transformation.

After working with Atousa on as many things as I wanted – she is always there for whatever you need, and you are actually driving the whole process because it is your own journey after all – I now see and experience a new way of embracing a life full of endless possibilities. The process also led me to see how my self-imposed disconnect from truly accepting a spiritual aspect in my life, whatever that means to me, combined with multiple rigid rules and unreasonably high expectations I was holding on to, didn't help me live my life in a fulfilling way for me. More than just feeling better about life in general, I am now more loving and accepting of myself.

With every new day, I see how this renewed version interacts with life in a more purposeful way and is more aware of the present moment. Others have experienced my change too. They may not even realize – they don't need to – but my more recent way of interreacting with others, with more openness and being more truthful to myself, often result in more smiles, laughs and connectedness than before. Now I am more relax and less analytical and critical about the little things in life, and conversations are lighter. All it takes me is to surrender to the present moment and be myself, be confident and trust myself. I repeat, trust myself. I am so happy with myself for giving this a try. It is as if my outer shell was destroyed and released to let me experience a new way of life.

Before, during a day like today, I would be wondering what's wrong with me or why can't I be as good as I think I should be, along with all the typical self-judgement we learn to accept from ourselves and others and that we learn starting very early in life.

Now, I simply embrace the present moment and better connect with everything and everyone around me. And I absolutely love, trust, and accept myself.

All it took was to step into Atousa's studio, follow her guidance to connect with myself (the process is similar to meditating or could be a conversation, depending on what it is that you are looking for), do my homework (yes, there is homework involved), and trust myself during the process. The most important part of the process, in my option, is to trust yourself and put the effort you require to achieve your own goals. If you got to this point by putting not much effort and work into yourself, you are not going to get unstuck by doing the same. Self-transformation is a process, generally including several steps and actions on your end, but it all leads to the other end of the rainbow – you just need to cross that bridge for yourself. And there is support and guidance for you to get there.

In addition to connecting and communicating better with others, even my day-to-day activities, and simple things in life, seem more special and even magical, including things we take for granted like breathing, for example. The calming feeling of air entering my airways, filling up my lungs, and slowly getting back out connects me with my body and make appreciate a moment of awareness in my body. Similarly, seeing the bees diligently doing their work while also helping provide food for the word, so effortlessly, is interesting, exciting, and magical.

As I experience this different way of life, others get to have new and better experiences with me too. Not only because I no longer carry worries and doubts that distanced me from others, but because it gets easier to connect with everyone and my help is more accessible to anyone this way. I see this magic when crossing paths with people who seem to be too different or incompatible with me at first instance. But as I no longer focus on the differences and better see past them, I get to find new ways to connect and interact as possible, without getting stuck.

I also find it easier to be helpful to others as I am no longer busy with thoughts of things I perceived as mistakes I've done or future worries. This helps me be more available to others. I get to share this new life and what I have learned with those around me. Transforming yourself has such an enormous impact in the world around you – you just have to be you, your transformed self.

My experience has been so transformative and radical that I recommend my brother, who is walking his own path in life, to reach out to Atousa. We are incredibly different in the way we view and describe the universe the surrounds us, but we have a strong connection and siblings.

He shared a few concerns he had about feeling stuck, and I quickly related to the feeling he was describing. It only took one conversation with Atousa for him to come back with advice he found useful, thoughtful, and informative on his very analytical perspective. Sharing this has brought us even closer. Now I learn from this example and from what he shares with me from this perspective. He is part of my journey now and helps me to continue growing and learning too – he even contributed to this testimonial.

We recently celebrated life during a sibling's weekend getaway. As we all get transformed, everything and everyone surrounding us shifts too.

What's next for me? I am most excited to find out as I continue going about my life. I trust I will make the best choices for me and others when the time comes, and that I can choose to change at any given moment. I surrender to the present moment and simply enjoy and experience life with all its magic, including mine. I embrace transformation as a way of life; not just as if it was this one-time item to be checked off a to-do list. A life full of possibilities is imbued with continuous transformation.

I think that a life transformation journey, whether it is a onetime activity or a life-long adventure, is for anyone who wants to embark on a process that will transform their lives. There are no prerequisites, or books to follow.

All you need is available to you and Atousa can help you identify and use those resources. Another resource is those around you and, along this stretch of my path, I have met wonderful people who have worked with Atousa. I'm thankful for crossing paths with them and for the opportunity to learn about their stories.

I am excited for the opportunity to share a bit of my amazing transformational journey with her. As I write this, I feel as if I am no longer the same person who reached out to Atousa two years ago for the first time. The way I experience life now is radically different.

I am so glad I reached out to Atousa and to be part of the wonderful people whose life she has changed. She is so kind and amazing to work with that she continues to be my go-to person for guidance and matters related to the services she provides. We are always growing and learning as we make our own paths. She is always there, just a message away.

Thank you for reading this short version of a chapter of my very extensive, exciting, and magical story. I wholeheartedly wish you find the answers you are seeking for, and that you get to transform yourself and experience the life your heart desires.

With love,
Daisy D.

SHONNA'S STORY

Transformation is defined as a dramatic thorough change in the form of appearance. But what if transformation goes deeper than that? What if transformation is to see yourself fully once again and to shed those layers of armor you placed on yourself because the world was scary? What if the weight of the world is really that armor *you* placed on yourself over the years?

Like many of us, I come from a very dysfunctional family and past. Resultantly, I implemented a 900-mile barrier between myself and my home state, thinking this would be the end of my chaos. However, physical work only gets you so far. Some things are so deeply rooted that we refuse to see that the issue is not just on the outside, but what we choose to carry and bury within ourselves.

I came to Atousa with the intention of becoming a shaman. I understood there was more to the physical world than what meets the eye. I have always been aware of the spiritual realm, higher power and more. from an early age. The paranormal was my second normal… So, when starting this chapter, I was eager to learn and dive deeper into becoming what I thought a healer was, ready to face what awaits this adventure. I soon discovered the path to becoming a shaman was unconditional love—love for that terrified little girl I left in my home state and that woman I buried under so much armor.

Atousa guided me to see that fear was one of my biggest obstacles. I never thought of myself as an emotional person, and I was very driven by my logic. I believed that doing the right, or good, thing was out of fairness. *To do what is good solely by others we are in turn not being fair to our individual selves.* I had immersed myself in the medical field, both human and animal, to employ 'helping' others as a way to distract myself from my own pain. My philosophy was that by healing others I would find my own personal healing without having to deal with it. Thus, I stretched myself thin and left very little of *me* for myself. I lost sight of who I was by placing these social *blinders* over my eyes. Consequently, I was neglecting my personal emotions, what I was needing from myself, and my overall spiritual health.

With every session, Atousa took the time to ease me into pulling back those layers of trauma to truly see and heal myself. There were a lot of ugly moments in my past that I blocked out and Atousa aided me in shifting my perspective. Greeting each memory, trigger, and fear with unconditional love - listening to what that past version of me was needing and releasing those 'forgotten' traumas instead of recoiling. As the weight of my traumas and armor were removed, I began to see more of me, more of who I was and who I have always been. I was already a healer. The dramatic change in appearance was nothing to do with my physical self. Part of my transformation was dropping everything that I carried, listening to what I was needing, and accepting myself fully. *Both the light and the dark are needed to see our full individual selves. We all have our shadows and that is what makes us solid beings.*

I discovered, while on this healing journey, that communication was my weakness and my greatest passion. During my childhood, I struggled with words often and was even placed in speech classes in grade school. I've realized now as an adult this was due to my traumatic past and having a family that kept my past under wraps. I can recall a time in my teens trying to express that I felt depressed, only to have my mother threaten to place me in a psych ward and my stepfather mock me. However, art was an outlet for this. This gave me the opportunity to communicate what I was feeling onto a canvas. I spoke silent speeches with every stroke. In addition to this as a child, I had a deep love for animals, and I see where I sympathized with these creatures that had no voice. A memory resurfaced during meditation one evening of myself as a child explaining that my desire one day was to become a painter and someone who spoke on behalf of animals due to them not having a voice; never wanting them to feel the way that I felt. This brought so many waves of emotions. Communication was and is my passion regardless of if I saw it, or not. The Universe knew what it was doing even if I did not understand it at the time.

Instead of viewing my past with a bitter taste and indigestible, I savored every flavor thoroughly. The Universe always has a plan and it wanted me to *transform* the perspective I had on my life. Every experience was out of love and when we start to neglect ourselves the Universe will crank up the level of the lesson. You want to go hard, the Universe will give you hard lessons.

When Atousa and I first started our journey, we had a plan, but the Universe had other things in mind. Instead of stopping to follow what we originally discussed we allowed my soul to speak. I understood the practice of Shamanism without formal training, most of it came second nature due to listening to my own guides. My transformation started when I stopped treating myself like crap, communicating with myself truthfully, and living honestly by the beat of my own drum. Loving unconditionally not just myself, but the whole picture even if I could not see above the horizon. There are days when I may get lost in the hustle, but through the lessons with Atousa, I tap that *pause* button and pull myself back. When this happens, I ask myself the most important questions: "How am I feeling? Does this feel good to me? What is my body telling me?" Then just listen—muting logical Shonna.

Healing may seem scary, but it only is if you allow it to be. Healing can be painful, but is it due to your own resistance to learning the lesson? Feel it out and *listen* to your heart, it has the best intention, and your past is the greatest master to tame the life that you once thought was a disaster.

To transform is not just defined as a complete physical change that can be seen. Transformation is also defined as looking at what you allowed yourself to hold onto, seeing it with unclouded eyes, and letting go. Just because it was a rainy day, it does not make it a bad day.

The most recent result of my work with Atousa showed me the power of unconditional love and communication. I was asked by an acquaintance to create a company logo for her jewelry business. I listened to not only what she was verbally explaining to me but what she was *communicating* to me. That night I drew up not only what she had verbally requested, but I also put other finer details that were not asked of me while keeping it simple and clean. I made sure to maintain the original design of the silhouette of a woman's face with a large afro-bun. However, I could see and hear that the bun had to sit a certain way, the color of the hair needed to be the galaxy, and rose quartz/amethyst needed to be the border. I know this may be a bit hard to picture with just words, but once the logo resonated with her energy I was finished.

When presenting her logo, I was met with tears. She explained to me that the year prior to opening her jewelry business, her grandmother passed. During the funeral she placed rose quartz beside her grandmother's body due to it being her grandmother's personal favorite, adding that amethyst was her own favorite. She further explained that when her grandmother was alive, they would admire the stars and that her grandmother always loved her natural messy afro-bun. She admitted that her grandmother was her biggest supporter, and witnessing her grandmother communicate with me to translate her love through this design touched her heart more than she could ever express. It was healing per her words.

The reason I chose to walk this path and transform my life is that *spiritual healing goes further than the surface. When we heal ourselves, we also heal the generations before us and after us. We heal our past lives, and we heal those who enter our lives with or without knowing.*

Shonna Ray Perkins

ABOUT THE AUTHOR

Atousa Raissyan, founder of Soulystic Healing Sanctuary, is recognized as a shaman, published author, heart-centered transformational healer, spiritual guide and teacher, digital artist, poet, inspirational speaker, life changer, and host of the podcast *Goodbye Bullshit, Hello Happiness*.

"Game-changer", "intuitive gifted healer", "guiding light", "life-changing", "magic", "a blessing", and "best teacher and mentor" are often how Atousa's clients describe their experience with her.

As a holistic health practitioner, she connects with her clients, their painful parts that are hiding in the darkness. Atousa helps her clients to reconnect with these parts to heal and reprogram their past experiences. Through different healing modalities, she helps to release the past, reconnect with their true nature, and assist in reprograming and realigning with universal energy and the source, which is love.

Atousa has been practicing the art of wellness for over seventeen years. During this time, her clients have expressed how she has transformed their lives and in turn their families' lives. Most of her clients have tried traditional and holistic/alternative practices without success and come to her once they have lost hope.

Atousa's work has helped clients transform their lives by releasing traumas, healing emotional and spiritual wounds, opening up new life paths through changed perspectives, habits and behaviors, and more. She helps her clients reach their goals, make their dreams a reality, and learn the skills to live a happier and more fulfilling life.

Working with Atousa is a practice of self-love and becoming more in tune with yourself and the world around you. Empowering you to elevate your life and live in harmony with your purpose.

She has extensive experience in, and passion for, helping individuals to discover and tap into their "true self", to unlock their potential to experience their desired life in abundance, relationship, and personal well-being.

Atousa believes that we are all an evolving work in progress. Her own transformation and healing journey has been her training ground to perfect the healing modalities that she uses for her clients today.

Her healing space provides a sanctuary for her clients to feel safe and at peace so that they can express themselves freely, knowing that they are not being judged and what they discuss with her stays confidential. Many clients share that by just walking into her space, they feel at ease and at peace, which is well suited for releasing and healing.

She is most proud of the positive impact she has made in her clients' lives, reflected in her client testimonials. She is most grateful to her clients for allowing her to be part of their journey. Atousa loves empowering them and seeing the progress that they have made from their initial visit. Each of her clients have a special place in her heart. She feels blessed to be their guide and to know that someday they will be healing others on their path.

She has been featured in USA Today, Potomac Lifestyle, Entrepreneurs Herald, Thrivers in Action, MENAFN, New Age Tarot Readings, and has been number one on Amazon Bestseller's List. In the past two years, she has been the featured speaker in over twenty-five podcasts and summits.

Websites: *www.AtousaRaissyan.com*
www.SoulysticArtShop.com
www.Etsy.com/shop/SoulysticApparelShop
Instagram: *@atousar, @soulystic, @BeLove_SeeLove*
Facebook: *@Soulystic*
YouTube: *@AtousaRaissyan*
Podcast: *Goodbye Bullshit, Hello Happiness*
LinkedIn: *www.linkedin.com/in/atousaraissyan*
Email: *ar.soulystic@gmail.com*
Phone/Text: *240-244-9321*

Made in the USA
Middletown, DE
22 August 2023